A CAVE
IN THE
CLOUDS

A Young Woman's Escape from ISIS

BADEEAH HASSAN AHMED

with **SUSAN ELIZABETH McCLELLAND**

annick press
toronto + berkeley

The spelling of Yazidi words in this book are based on transliterations of the Shingali, Kurdish, and Arabic languages. Badeeah's own name is a transliteration, and in previous media reports has also been spelled "Badia." We tried to remain as authentic to the transliteration into English of the Shingali language as possible.

Cover designed by Emma Dolan
Interior designed by Kong Njo
Edited by Barbara Pulling

Photo on facing page depicts Badeeah's home in Kocho following the ISIS attack in 2014.
Maps © pop_jop / iStockphoto.com modified by Paul Covello

Annick Press Ltd.

We acknowledge the support of the Canada Council for the Arts, the Ontario Arts Council, and the Government of Canada through the Canada Book Fund (CBF) for our publishing activities.

 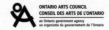

Cataloging in Publication

Ahmed, Badeeah Hassan, author
    A cave in the clouds : a young woman's escape from ISIS / Badeeah Hassan Ahmed with Susan Elizabeth McClelland.

Issued in print and electronic formats.
ISBN 978-1-77321-235-7 (hardcover).–ISBN 978-1-77321-234-0 (softcover).–
ISBN 978-1-77321-237-1 (HTML).–ISBN 978-1-77321-236-4 (PDF)

    1. Ahmed, Badeeah Hassan. 2. Ahmed, Badeeah Hassan--Kidnapping, 2014.
3. Kidnapping victims–Iraq–Biography. 4. Iraq–History–2003-. 5. Yazidi–
Crimes against–Iraq. 6. Women–Crimes against–Iraq. 7. IS (Organization).
I. McClelland, Susan, author II. Title.

DS70.8.Y49A36 2019   956.7044'3092   C2018-905052-7
                                                    C2018-905053-5

Published in the U.S.A. by Annick Press (U.S.) Ltd.
Distributed in Canada by University of Toronto Press.
Distributed in the U.S.A. by Publishers Group West.

Printed in Canada

www.annickpress.com
www.smcclelland.com

Also available as an e-book. Please visit annickpress.com/ebooks for more details.

To Adlan
and to my family,
Kocho, and
the Yazidi people

Contents

Foreword   vii

A Note from the Authors   xi

Maps   xiii

Chapter One: **The Purpose of Life**   3

Chapter Two: **Spoils of War**   15

Chapter Three: **The Stranger**   26

Chapter Four: **Invasion**   41

Chapter Five: **Sabaya**   51

Chapter Six: **Prisoner**   62

Chapter Seven: **Adrift**   70

Chapter Eight: **On the Other Side**   79

Chapter Nine: **In Between Heaven and Earth**   87

Chapter Ten: **Awakening**   99

Chapter Eleven: **Immortal**   108

Chapter Twelve: **The Dark Room** 113

Chapter Thirteen: **The American** 119

Chapter Fourteen: **A Cave in the Clouds** 130

Chapter Fifteen: **Jinn** 136

Chapter Sixteen: **Death** 149

Chapter Seventeen: **Houses** 156

Chapter Eighteen: **Reunion** 164

Chapter Nineteen: **Escape** 170

Chapter Twenty: **Return to Iraq** 180

Chapter Twenty-One: **We're Not Afraid of Darkness** 194

Chapter Twenty-Two: **Return to Love** 206

Chapter Twenty-Three: **Giving** 212

Chapter Twenty-Four: **Freedom** 216

Epilogue 228

Acknowledgments 230

Foreword

The Yazidi people are an ethnic and religious minority in the Middle East, with their largest population concentrated in Northern Iraq. Yazidis are Kurmanji-speaking and practice a monotheistic religion that reflects a spectrum of teachings and beliefs from various other religions including Gnostic Christianity, Judaism, Sufi Islam, and Zoroastrianism. Rather than formal ceremonies, their religious practice involves visiting sacred places. Yazidis participate in baptisms and feasts, sing hymns, and recite stories. Some of their stories are about historical and mythical battles fought in protection of the religion. Others, told over the centuries by generations of women, detail methods of resistance to the same threats that Yazidi women face today. The Yazidi people believe that they are descended solely from Adam, that angels guard the world, that reincarnation is possible, and that there is no distinction between heaven and hell. Because these beliefs vary significantly from other religions, the Yazidis have been targeted throughout history and persecuted by Muslim rulers in the region who demanded that they convert to Islam. Yazidis have been labelled "devil worshipers," "infidels," and "non-believers." These labels have, for centuries, served as the foundation of efforts to destroy Yazidi communities and alienated the Yazidis from other groups. Over the course of their history, the Yazidis have suffered and survived seventy-four separate genocidal attacks.[1]

More recently, the Yazidis were made vulnerable by forced displacement under Saddam Hussein; the economic meltdown of Iraq under UN sanctions; the breakdown of the state and security after the US-led invasion of 2003; and the political failures that followed. In Iraq, there are now around 500,000 Yazidis, primarily from the Sinjar region in Nineveh province in the country's north. The Yazidis of Syria and Turkey have mostly fled to neighboring countries or to Europe.

The Islamic State of Iraq and Syria (also known as ISIS and by its Arabic language acronym, Daesh) waged a targeted attack against the Yazidi people in Iraq in August 2014. The systematic sexually-based violence organized by ISIS against Yazidi women and girls commenced immediately. Most of the women and girls were forced into holding cells where they witnessed and experienced sexual assault as ISIS members "selected" women as unwilling partners or else sold them into sexual slavery. They were treated like property as they were assessed on appearance and then bought, sold, traded, and gifted between extensive networks of ISIS fighters throughout Iraq and Syria. UN findings illustrate the high emotional and psychological needs of these women, even after they've successfully escaped or been rescued from ISIS. Years later, women and girls are still considered the most vulnerable population of Yazidi refugees.

Many Yazidi women are still hoping for the day when they can give their testimony as part of an official process to hold ISIS accountable for their crimes against humanity. As one anonymous victim has said, "It has been four years. We want to record everything that happened so it can be used as evidence. We are waiting."[2] By telling her story and bringing the experiences of Yazidi women to light, Badeeah is actively participating in this long-sought-after process of sharing and healing—revealing what has been in her heart since the first moment her village was attacked.

Yazidi women are not archetypal victims or heroes. They are individual human beings who have experienced atrocious crimes but who also made active decisions for their survival and protection, ultimately defying their perpetrators. As Adlan speaks to Badeeah during her time in captivity, "Always move to the light. Don't let the darkness in. Hold onto love, so that darkness will eventually be banished." Together, Yazidi women and girls have continued to preserve their religion, instill a sense of pride in their children and community, and speak out for oppressed people all over the world. Together, we will banish the darkness.

—Nafiya Naso, founder of the Canadian Yazidi Association and founding member of Operation Ezra.

Operation Ezra was founded to increase general awareness about the plight of the Yazidi people in the Middle East and to raise funds for the sponsorship of Yazidi refugee families to Winnipeg, Canada. To date, they have helped resettle dozens of Yazidi refugees. This project was set in motion by the Jewish Community in Winnipeg and has grown to include people from all walks of life.

[1] Canada. Parliament. House of Commons. Standing Committee on Citizenship and Immigration. (July 2016). *Evidence*. 24th Report. 42nd Parliament, 1st Session. Available: www.ourcommons.ca/DocumentViewer/en/42-1/CIMM/ meeting-24/evidence.

[2] Marczak , Nikki. "All the Survivors Have a Book inside Their Hearts." *SBS World News Online*, SBS, 3 Aug. 2018, www.sbs.com.au/topics/life/culture/article/2018/08/01/ all-survivors-have-book-inside-their-hearts.

A Note from the Authors

Badeeah Hassan Ahmed and writer Susan Elizabeth McClelland first met in the summer of 2016. At that time, Susan was asked by the magazine *Marie Claire* UK to write a story on a female survivor of the Yazidi genocide. Susan worked with translator Sozan Fahmi to research potential subjects. Badeeah's story stood out from every other account that had been in the press. Among other things, Badeeah's story spoke to the sacrifices so many Yazidi women and girls had made to help others at the risk of their own deaths. And her abduction shed light on a startling fact: in Syria, it is estimated that the majority of Daesh fighters (otherwise known as ISIS) are in fact foreign born and/or citizens of Western countries.

When Badeeah first escaped Aleppo and it was discovered that it was an American, possibly a commander, who had taken her, she was flown to the United States. There, she gave talks at conferences about the genocide and worked with the US State Department to try to identify her captor. It was hard for Badeeah to relive her trauma at the hands of Daesh. But Badeeah realized that her story could bring international attention to the crisis experienced by the Yazidi people. She agreed to turn her story into a book in the hopes of reaching an even wider audience, so more people could know the truth of what is still happening in Syria.

Over the course of a year, Badeeah, Sozan, and Susan worked together to retell Badeeah's story. They consulted closely with members of the Yazidi community, including Dakhill Shammo, Nasir Kiret, and Imad and Fawaz Farhan, to accurately and sensitively reflect Yazidi culture and spirituality. It was very important to them not only to tell a story of captivity and of war and survival but also to highlight the resilience of a culture unknown to many around the world.

But Badeeah's is also a difficult story to tell. Because so much happened during the course of her captivity, it was impossible to chronicle every detail. In writing this book for young readers, some creative license has been taken to compensate for this, including reconstructing the order of events, combining some characters, and recreating dialogue where necessary.

Today Badeeah and Eivan and his mother live in Germany. Badeeah is determined to become a nurse and give back to her people. *A Cave in the Clouds* is Badeeah's story: it is not just about war and what it does to women and girls; it is about the restorative power of storytelling and the remarkable human ability to find meaning even in the darkest of times.

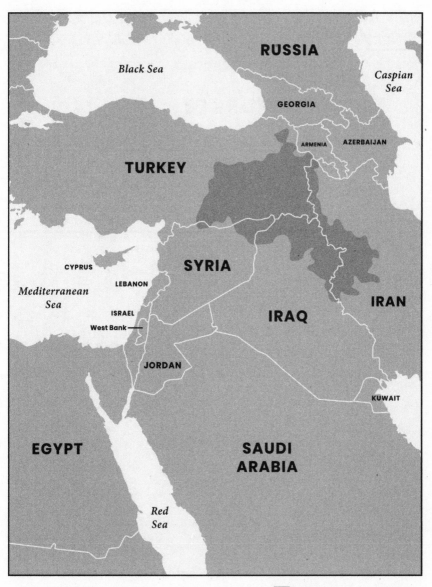

KURDISTAN REGION

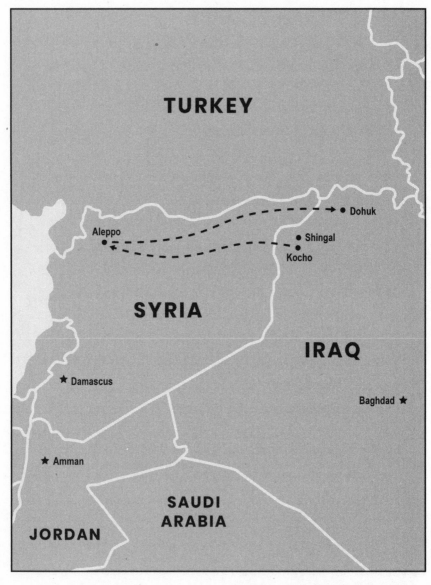

August 15, 2014

The walls of our house shook.

Trucks roared down the road. Some were sparkling white, with missile launchers in the cargo beds. Some were armored trucks with long gun barrels.

I ran.

Suddenly, I wasn't in Kocho anymore but in a thick forest of Zagros oak trees. I seemed to be in the hills near the Turkish border. A man was chasing me, calling out in a language I recognized from news reports as English.

Then it was no longer day. The only light came from a half-moon behind a thin veil of clouds. I tripped and fell, hitting my head on a rock. My head throbbed with pain, but I scrambled to get up. The man was approaching fast.

I called out for help, but all that came back to me was my own voice bouncing off the rocks.

Soon I was running again, until I spotted Eivan. He was slumped beside a stream, as if leaning into the water to play. I was so happy to see him. But as I neared, I realized that he wasn't playing at all but was asleep, with one hand in the stream. The other was twisted behind his back, as if it was broken. I screamed.

Chapter One

August 2003

The Purpose of Life

It was August, near the end of summer holidays in our village of Kocho. My father and my older brothers and sisters were all on vacation. The Forty Days of Heat we call Chilé Haviné, which starts on June 24 and stretches until August 2, had ended. During Chilé Haviné, daytime temperatures in Iraq can soar to over 50 degrees Celsius (122 degrees Fahrenheit). After that, the cooler temperatures roll in.

That morning, my sisters Hadil and Majida awoke while it was still dark, curled and pinned up their hair, and put on their good dresses. They'd washed and mended them the day before with the help of our *dake*, our grandmother. My sisters were going to the market with our father, Hassan, in a rusty pickup truck he had borrowed from his brother.

It was 2003. The Americans had been in our country for just a few months, and Iraq's former president, the dictator Saddam Hussein, was in hiding. We Yazidi people were freer than we had been in generations. Under Saddam, there had been no national elections. He and his party, called Ba'ath, had appointed whomever they wanted to hold important positions. Those positions were mostly given to men of the same religion as Saddam, Sunni Muslims, and rarely to Shi'ite Muslims or any minority group, including the Yazidi. Now our country was moving toward democracy and having people vote in their leaders. My father, Hassan, was running to be the local representative for the Kurdistan Democratic Party.

But on this day, as he prepared to go to market, he was Hassan the farmer.

I watched as he loaded our neighbor's truck with boxes of eggplant, green peppers, tomatoes, onions, and zucchinis we'd grown on our nearby farm. Hassan sold our fruits and vegetables in Shingal, about a 20-kilometer (12-mile) drive away. Kocho, which had a population of 1,785, was an entirely Yazidi village. Shingal was a mix of Yazidi, Kurds, and Arabs. The Yazidi have lived in northwestern Iraq for thousands of years, stretching all the way back to the ancient civilizations there, including the Sumerians. Christian and Jewish populations lived here, too. But under Saddam Hussein, our region had become increasingly Arab. Saddam's army had invaded many Yazidi villages, forcing the inhabitants out and moving the Arabs, his own people, in.

Hadil and Majida hopped into the truck and closed the passenger door. My heart exploded. I was desperate to go with them. They weren't just going to the Shingal market. Hadil was old enough to go to school now so they were also going to the city to collect her Jinsiya, or identity papers. Majida, who was ten, already attended. Kocho only had a primary school. Many Yazidi families in Iraq didn't send their children to school because the history and religion taught there was Islamic and the classes were in Arabic, and they feared losing their culture. But my parents believed in education.

Hadil and Majida, chattering like cockatiels, had taunted me the night before, saying they both would be at school soon while I was home caring for our baby brother, Khudher. Khudher, three years younger than me, was hard work. When my mother, Adlan, came to the farm with us, I was put in charge of him while she tended the crops. Khudher wouldn't sit still, not ever. The moment I turned my back on him, he'd scamper off, hiding in the plants and bushes. Hadil teased that while she was with our cousins at school every day, I would be learning to bake bread and cook *dolma* (meat, rice, and vegetables wrapped in leaves) and *kubbeh* (a meat dish made with spices and wheat). I hated cooking.

A breeze blew around me, carrying sweet perfume from the blossoms of our dake's orange trees in her yard next door. As with most Yazidi families in Kocho, my father had built his house next to his parents'.

That morning, the scented air didn't comfort me like it usually did.

I scowled and tapped my foot.

My mother pushed her way past me, the hem of her white dress sweeping the ground. As usual, locks of her gray hair slipped out from underneath her *kufi*, the white cap older women wear. She marched up to the truck and poked her head through the open window, reminding my sisters to bring back some black pepper and cumin for soups. "You forgot last time you went to Shingal, interested only in buying fabric for dresses," she scolded.

Majida brushed our mother away. Adlan clicked her tongue and shook her head. Majida was defiant. One of our older brothers, Fallah, said Majida was political, which was dangerous for this part of the world and especially dangerous for a ten-year-old Yazidi girl. Hadil, on the other hand, was carefree. She reminded me of a bird, one of the nightingales that nested in an olive tree outside our house. Fallah said I wasn't like Hadil. I was responsible and careful. I talked little, but when I did, my words really meant something. Fallah said I wasn't like Majida, either. She was sullen.

Fallah had taken me aside on Charshama Sorr or Red Wednesday, the Yazidi New Year, which occurs on the first day of the Yazidi calendar: the first Wednesday between April 14 and 21. "You see beauty where others don't," he told me. We were celebrating the New Year at Sharfabeen, a temple on the south side of the Shingal Mountains. Sharfabeen and Lalish, a village in the rolling hills near the border of Kurdistan, are Yazidi holy places. We Yazidi believe Lalish is the center of the earth, where the earth itself was formed, and we walk barefoot through the village to absorb its spiritual energy. Lalish, some say, is half a million years old.

That particular night, as we celebrated the New Year at Sharfabeen, people were gathered around fires, eating goat and gossiping. The young people were dancing. Dake, wrinkled like the sand at ninety-five, was barely able to move, her bones hardened like cement, but she sat on a cushion and watched. Many people approached her to kiss her hands, to honor her strength and wisdom. When the fires were at their brightest, I told Fallah that in Dake's eyes, inky as a moonless night, I could see her dancing, as if she was enjoying an inner world of stars and music.

Fallah smiled at me. He said I was bold, too, when I wanted to be.

That morning, watching Majida and Hadil waiting to go to Shingal, was one of those times.

I crept toward the truck and peered in. Majida and Hadil were fussing with each other's hair. They both had long, dark-brown hair, like mine, which they brushed sometimes a hundred times a night, so it was silky and straight. I spied an opening in the back seat between the boxes of fruit and vegetables, a space big enough for tiny me, I thought.

I slipped over to the driver's side. I reached for the handle and pulled. But as I pried open the door, it squeaked, startling my father, who was now loading okra from his brother Khalil's farm into the truck's cargo bed.

"What are you doing, Badeeah?" he called. My mother's voice was bright and full, reminding me of the marigolds that danced in Dake's garden, but Hassan's voice was deep and throaty. It made me think of the wild water buffalo that used to live in the marshes of Iraq before Saddam Hussein had the marshes drained to punish those who sought to overthrow him.

"I want to come," I said nervously. My father walked over to stand right in front of me. I had to crane my neck to see his face. When he was on holidays or working at the farm, Hassan wore clothes similar to those of our Muslim or Arab neighbors in nearby villages: *dishdashas* and *khaftans*. But when he was out canvasing to be a politician, he wore a traditional Yazidi costume, with a checkered red-and-white turban called a Jamadani. Hassan's hands, leathered and calloused, were on his hips. His trim beard was more salt than pepper.

I liked being close to my father, which I often wasn't. I shared him with my four older brothers, my younger brother, Khudher, my five older sisters, and also all of Kocho, it seemed. Adlan said that while our family was from the lowest caste, the Merids, our father did such important work that he was well respected even among the high castes, the Sheikhs and the Pirs. Castes mattered, especially in marriages. In the late afternoon, Hassan would sit in the room of our home reserved for male guests, his legs tucked underneath him, as the other men from the village dropped in to talk politics. My father would smoke hand-rolled cigars and cigarettes while his visitors smoked the *shisha* pipe. Adlan had long, thin hands that glided in the air when she spoke, like the outstretched wings of a hawk. With those hands, she would shoo me away from listening to Hassan and the village men. "They talk of violence and blood," she would tell me, pushing me toward the kitchen.

The candies and chocolate biscuits Adlan gave me, along with the stories she told, made me soon forget Hassan and his guests. Most of the time, I felt unworthy of my father's attention.

But not this time.

On this day, I stood like an ant in front of my father's dusty, black boots, my heart racing. I crossed my arms and looked up at him. "I want to come," I repeated, my voice croaking from nerves. "I want to go to school."

"You're too young to go to school," Hassan said, bending down. I could smell him now, cigarette smoke and the outdoors, dry earth after rain.

"But I want to go now," I said. "And I want to see Shingal. Everyone has been there but me. I want to learn things." A tear dropped down my cheek. Images of myself doing math equations and learning Arabic, the language most widely spoken in Iraq, were starting to fade. I knew in my heart I was meant to start school, but I didn't have the words to convince Hassan. I watched an ant scurry along the ground. The little ant seemed much stronger than me.

"Okay," my father said, stretching himself up.

I jumped with surprise.

"The teacher at the school in Kocho may not accept you for another year or two, but we'll get your identity card and try. Majida and Hadil," he bellowed, "move over. Badeeah is coming with us."

We bumped along the desert highway, swerving around the potholes Hassan spotted, flying over the others that had crept up on him too fast. Majida and Hadil were discussing the store in the market that sold fresh juices. Orange was Hadil's favorite. Coconut was Majida's. I knew my sisters were rubbing it in that they had visited Shingal and I hadn't.

I ignored them.

My father talked, to no one in particular, about how at least now our identity cards said we were Yazidi. When Saddam led the country, many families refused to get identification cards because their nationality was listed as Arab. And since many Yazidi women gave birth to their babies at home, children also didn't have birth certificates. That was how Adil, my eldest brother, landed on the frontlines of the first American invasion of Iraq in 1991 at the age of sixteen. The army thought he was older than he was, and since he didn't have any identification to prove otherwise, they forced him into battle.

I watched with excitement as the Shingal mountain range rose up around us, the weeds tumbling along the desert floor and birds flying alongside. Hassan put a Kurdish radio station on, as the only news available now came to the area by satellite from Kurdistan. Majida and Hadil sang along to the songs they recognized.

As our truck rolled into the city and joined what seemed like a thousand cars and trucks all honking at the same time, Hassan turned off the radio and my sisters finally fell quiet. I had never seen so many people before: young men on motorbikes that farted thick, black smoke, older men driving rusty trucks, vendors hawking newspapers and electronics, women with their heads covered by long scarves that flapped in the air like flags.

"Muslim women wear *hijabs*, head coverings, or *khimars*, that cover not only the head but also most of the body," Majida informed me in a haughty voice. "We don't." What a know-it-all. I rolled my eyes and looked out the window.

Our truck stopped, stuck in traffic, beside a woman sitting on a tattered blue blanket on the edge of the road. She was covered in black in what Majida said was a khimar and *niqab* set. The woman held a sign in Arabic, which I asked Hassan to translate:

I am poor. I am a war widow. My husband was a martyr, a shahid. I have two small children to care for and no family to take me in. Please help.

With her other hand, the woman shook a tin can. I could hear the rattle of *dinar*, Iraqi currency, and so I reached into the little shelf underneath the radio and grabbed some coins. I was opening the door to give them to her when Hassan stepped on the gas.

"Why did you do that?" I yelled, slamming the door closed. "She needs money. Her husband was a martyr."

"It's not safe," he said quietly as we sped by some serious-looking men walking in twos along the side of the road. I knew they were soldiers. I recognized the blue-and-black uniform of the new Iraqi government army, who were fighting the guerilla groups opposing the Americans. The Kurds also had an army, called Peshmerga, who protected Shingal and our villages now.

Majida and Hadil lowered their heads, nervously tying and untying the ends of the scarves they had wrapped around their shoulders. Their actions reminded me of a ritual we did when we visited Lalish. The tomb of one of the Yazidi saints, the twelfth-century mystic Sheikh Adi ibn Musafir, is located in one of the three main buildings at Lalish. Whenever we visited, we would tie knots in the fabric draped over his tomb. As we did so, we would pray.

But I didn't think Majida and Hadil were praying on this day. I thought they were scared.

"Are we going to have another war?" I asked my father.

"There is always war," Hassan said, wiping his perspiring forehead with the back of his hand. He, too, seemed anxious, which wasn't like him. "Right now, the enemies are terrorists, including the group al-Qaeda. They hate that the Americans are here."

"Adlan says we Yazidi are special," I continued, ignoring Hadil, who was slapping my thigh to get me to be quiet. She didn't like it when I was the center of attention. "Adlan says we're one of the oldest peoples in the world. She says our enemies are afraid of the knowledge that we bring with us from the beginning of time."

Hassan steered the truck to the side of the road. He sat looking forward for what felt like ages, then turned off the ignition.

"If we're so special, why do people want to hurt us?" I pressed on.

"Everyone is special," Hassan said. The color that had drained from his face was returning.

"Adlan says that everyone has light inside of them. Is that what it means to be special?"

"I guess so." Hassan leaned over to look at me and smiled.

"But I don't know what this light is," I said. "I've never seen it."

I could tell from my father's wrinkled forehead that he was thinking hard about his answer. "The light we're talking about isn't a color," he said finally. "It is like a feeling, like love. Not just the love of your family or even of yourself. That's almost a selfish love. But love that abounds and never ends and brings us together. In the dead of night, love is your compass. Many people's minds become deluded. They go crazy and forget about love, but it's always there, even in the darkest corners. Our purpose in life is to hold onto love, so that darkness will eventually be succeeded by morning."

Hassan hopped out of the truck and motioned for Majida, Hadil, and me to follow him. The city wasn't what I had expected. Gasoline fumes hung over it like a tent. And the dust! Country dust just made our dresses dirty. City dust was thick, coarse, and oily. It clogged my nose and throat and stung my eyes.

As I coughed, I thought about what Hassan had said. It sounded a bit like a riddle. Eleven years later, I would discover the reality of what my father had told me that day in Shingal. Light would guide me home after I became one of the Islamic State's *sabaya*, a prisoner of war.

Chapter Two

August 2, 2014

Spoils of War

"'To the victor belongs the spoils.' I think that's what Allah says about war booty and sabaya."

My brother Fallah's voice was hoarse from all his talking. It was late. He was sitting cross-legged on the rug beside Hassan in the guest room of our house. Adlan, Majida, and Hadil served him and the other men black tea in clear glasses, biscuits, and nuts. In contrast to the men, the women and girls seemed calm, moving like reeds of grass.

I was sitting on the windowsill eavesdropping.

Fallah and his three-year-old son, my nephew Eivan, were visiting us for summer holidays. They lived in Shingal, where Fallah was a police officer. Tonight was August 2, the end of Chilé Haviné. As a family, we had planned to visit the gravesites of relatives who had died, including Dake, my grandmother, that afternoon. But only the women and children had gone. The men had set off to search for Delshan, who worked for my cousin Nadia's family. Some sheep Delshan was minding had been stolen a few days earlier. Now Delshan himself was missing. He had been taken away by armed men no one recognized. Hassan, Fallah, and Adil had carried their own guns with them as they traveled to the Arab villages that surrounded Kocho. Delshan was nowhere to be found. Now the men were back, arguing over what to do next.

As I grew older and understood more of what Hassan and the other men talked about in our guest room, I discovered that war, always war, was first and foremost in their minds. Like my brother Adil, Fallah had been forced into the Iraqi army. Before that, Fallah had wanted to go into law or politics, like Hassan, who had succeeded first in one election and then another. Before Fallah became a soldier, his smile could light up a room. His dark eyes sparkled. He told jokes and made us all laugh. Now, he was cold to look at most of the time; his fire and warmth were buried so far down they often seemed lost to him.

Fallah was telling the men that Daesh, the Islamic State of Iraq and the Levant, known as ISIS in America, was responsible for Delshan's kidnapping. Daesh had entered Iraq from Syria and taken over the city of Fallujah, which was close to Baghdad, Iraq's largest city. Now Daesh had captured another city, Mosul, just 100 kilometers (62 miles) away from Kocho. Many of the Daesh men in Iraq were either former prisoners freed by Daesh from Iraqi jails or extremist Sunni Muslims wanting to continue Saddam Hussein's reign of terror, Fallah said.

I looked out at the road. The turmeric-colored sand mixed with rubble had settled from the convoy's return from searching for Delshan. The men in the guest room were smoking one cigarette after another.

"Daesh has taken over the Mosul dam and an oil refinery," Fallah continued. His nostrils flared and his fists were clenched tight.

Adil broke in. "They're launching an attack on Shingal from Baach and Bilich and other Sunni Muslim towns in the east and south." After my eldest brother was forced to join the Iraqi army, he never left. His most recent position had been guarding the Iraqi-Syrian border. But when Daesh breezed over the border the previous spring, Adil and his army colleagues had been captured and imprisoned in Baghdad. After his release, Adil returned to Kocho to help protect us.

"It's not safe for anyone," Fallah said, in a pleading voice. "We need to escape to the mountains."

"*Agh,*" said my father as he waved Fallah's concerns away. I could hear in Hassan's voice that he was tired. Tired of the talk of war, maybe. "It's nothing more than rumors. We've dealt with far worse. We will be safe."

"We should at least get the women and children out," my uncle Khalil protested.

"I agree," Adil snapped, banging a fist against the cement wall. Adil's gun, like the other men's guns, was propped up by the door alongside the mats Hassan kept there in case he had Arab guests over during the Muslim call to prayer. The AK-47s looked like firewood placed by a hearth. I knew that most of the guns had been bought secondhand in Mosul.

My father sighed, repeating that he wasn't concerned. Daesh was a Sunni and Shi'ite Muslim problem, he said. "Under Saddam, the Sunnis had the most power. Now the Shi'ites are in control of the government. This new war is between the two of them. Daesh just wants the Sunnis back running the country. Nothing to do with us."

The night song of the crickets was particularly loud that evening, probably due to the heat. It wasn't breaking as quickly as it usually did at the end of Chilé Haviné. During the burning Iraqi summers, we all waited for the winds to pick up so we could enjoy going out in the daytime again.

Fallah was talking now in a strained voice about his wife, Samira, Eivan's mother. She had gone to her family's village, Tal Banat, for a funeral. Fearing Daesh, Samira and her parents had decided to head into the Shingal Mountains to hide. Samira had told Fallah she would call when she was safe, but there hadn't been a call. Some men had heard reports that Daesh were killing Yazidi or taking them as prisoners as they tried to escape to the mountains. Fallah was desperate to leave and find Samira, but Adil reminded him he would be no good to his wife or his son if he were dead.

Hassan repeated again that everyone was overreacting. Back and forth they went . . .

I knew I would be told to leave if I spoke up, but I wanted to remind Fallah that cell phones didn't always work in the mountains. Whenever we visited Lalish, I would take long walks in the dry savannas. I always searched for caves in the mountains while I was there. It was in the caves, Adlan had told me, that the great Yazidi mystics came to understand God, which we refer to as the engineer of the universe. A few years earlier, I'd lost my way on one of those walks. When I tried to call my family for help, I discovered my phone didn't work. I couldn't find my way back. I was terrified, circling the same path over and over again. I finally knelt down and prayed to the chief of God's seven angels, Tawsi Malak, known also as Tawûsê Melek or Melek Taus, for the wisdom to find my way back. When a butterfly floated in front of me, I felt the urge to follow it. It led me out into a clearing, and from there, I found my way back to Lalish.

"Daesh are nothing but angry men," my father argued, bringing me back to the present. "They're not real Muslims, just like Saddam wasn't. They use Islam to fuel their selfish wants. They're not a threat to us."

The men all began to talk at once.

My mind drifted away again. Far, far away this time but not to the caves. I thought instead of Nafaa.

∾

Nafaa was two years older than me, a distant cousin on my father's side. He often came by our home to share a meal or to hang out with my brother Khudher. Nafaa and I had recently fallen in love, and when it turned warm, we would sneak out to the fields, spread a blanket on the ground, gaze up at the clouds, and talk about our futures. He wanted to get married one day. I did, too, when I was older.

"There's a turtle," Nafaa said one afternoon, pointing at a cloud. "It symbolizes movement and change . . . our journey together."

I play-slapped him, calling him a romantic. But secretly, I liked it when he talked to me like this.

The last time Nafaa and I had seen each other was at a spring wedding. Benyan, the groom, was the nephew of the head of Kocho, a man named Ahmed Jasso. Ahmed Jasso was responsible for things in our village, like a mayor in a North American city. But Ahmed Jasso hadn't been elected to his position. He was born into it. His official title was *mukhtar*. His father had been mukhtar and so had his grandfather.

The wedding stretched over a week, starting with Benyan's father asking the family of the bride, Nazma, for permission for the couple to wed. When Nazma and her family said yes, Benyan's family paid a bride price, in gold, given to the bride's parents to show how much respect the groom's family had for their new daughter-in-law.

On another night, the bride's hands were hennaed.

The festivities built up until the night of the main party.

I wore a pale lavender dress with gold embroidery to the party. I curled my hair and then pinned it up in the front, with the back worn long and loose, stretching nearly to my waist. Majida and Hadil did my makeup: coral and dusty-blue eye shadow, eyes lined in kohl, mascara, and lipstick. When they were done, Hadil said I looked like the Kurdish singer and actress Helly Luv, who has high cheekbones, a square jaw, big eyes, and a tiny frame. Of all my sisters, I was the smallest: five-foot-two and thin, 100 pounds at my heaviest.

I waved Hadil off. "Helly Luv is beautiful," I exclaimed. "I'm plain."

"You're not," Hadil said, standing back to admire her makeup job. "If you lived in Erbil, you could be on TV. Maybe you'll be the first Yazidi fashion model."

"I want to be a doctor," I protested.

"You can be both!" Majida raised her fist. Majida, who'd grown into a tomboy, big-boned and strong muscled, loved Helly Luv because she was also an activist. Her breakout hit, "Risk It All," was about women, the Kurds, the Yazidi—anyone who was oppressed.

Hadil hummed the song, spinning around on her tiptoes.

"We live in the new Iraq built by the Americans and Helly Luv," Hadil enthused, "where girls can be more than daughters, wives, and mothers. We can be anything!"

Majida gave Hadil a disdainful look. "We Yazidi already know that because of Mayan Khatun," she said in that know-it-all tone. Mayan Khatun was a Yazidi princess who became regent for her six-year-old grandson, Mir Tahsin Beg, in 1913, when the Yazidi were emerging from hundreds of years of persecution by the Ottomans. War and death were all around us then, too, and the Yazidi men were taking out their pain on their families, abusing their wives and children. As leader of the Yazidi people, Mayan Khatun taught us that we could not triumph against our oppressors until the balance of male and female among us was restored. Neither male nor female should be dominant in a society, she said. Each was a powerful energy. Under her leadership, the Yazidi launched several successful battles that eventually saw the Ottomans withdraw from our area. Because of her courage and wisdom, Mayan Khatun holds an important place in Yazidi history.

"Okay," I said with a shrug. "But my *anything* is to be a doctor."

The evening of Benyan and Nazma's wedding was warm. Hyacinths, roses, and lilacs were in bloom, dousing the air with their fragrance.

The party was held in Kocho, outside, on the street. In

front of the groom's house stretched tables of rice, beef dishes, pastries, and cakes.

By the time I arrived, musicians had already started playing music on framed drums, tamburs, and flutes.

After kissing the bride, I pinned a piece of gold to the groom's jacket lapel, which was my gift to the couple. My sisters slipped off to find their friends. Adlan joined the older women, who had lots of gossiping to do. Hassan gathered with the older men to smoke pipes. The men tried to not talk about war and politics at weddings. But without war and politics, they had little to say to one another.

My eyes searched the crowd, landing on some of the young men linking arms in the Dilan, our traditional Yazidi dance. I scanned their faces.

Nafaa was not among them.

My heart skipped when I finally spotted him kicking a football back and forth with Khudher. His wavy, chestnut hair had been brushed and oiled straight. He wore skinny, European-style brown suit pants and a tailored white button-down shirt open at the top. My heart started to beat fast. As if sensing me, he turned around, and our eyes locked.

For most of the night, wherever I moved, I felt Nafaa's gaze trailing me.

Yazidi teenagers don't date. Most brides and grooms meet at weddings or at Lalish, where many families visit several times a year, especially in the fall to celebrate our main festival, the Jazhna Jamaye.

Adlan had told me when I was little that every child enters this world with special gifts. "It's the mother's job," she said, "to help her children discover their gifts and cultivate them, the way we do our plants." The last time I had been to Lalish, I discovered my treasured gift. When I walked through the temple carrying Chira, a burning wick that we call the sacred fire, which is made from Lalish olive oil, I could sometimes see the future, as if I were a seer. What made my gift so exciting was that Nafaa always appeared beside me in my premonitions.

As night fell on Nazma and Benyan's wedding party, music played from a stereo.

The heavy bass made the ground vibrate. Men and women, girls and boys now linked arms, and the Dilan line wove its way around the street like a snake.

My arm was linked through Nafaa's.

Overhead, the clear sky stretched on forever.

I could see the Big Dipper and the Milky Way.

Around and around and around I spun.

Bang!

My father's fist slammed down hard on the tray in front of him, rattling the tea glasses. "Badeeah," he shouted.

I jumped down off the windowsill.

"Come and take Eivan."

Eivan had round eyes, rosy cheeks, and a cowlick that hung low on his forehead like an upside-down question mark. His giggles filled a room. Eivan was kneeling in front of Fallah, trying to get his father's attention. But all Fallah wanted was to talk about war.

I swooped my nephew into my arms and flew him like an airplane into the kitchen, where Hadil and Majida were eating kubbeh.

"Are you hungry?" I asked him as I landed him in between my sisters. He shook his head.

"Tell me a story." He reached up and twirled strands of my hair around his fingers.

"In a bit," I said, sitting down behind him. "I need to eat."

"The men scare me."

I felt his tiny body tensing and pulled him in close. "Don't listen to the men's talk. You'll learn soon enough that they make mountains out of ant hills. They exaggerate everything. You're safe here with me."

Eivan let me feed him some *naan,* a type of flatbread. As I watched him eat, a wave of sadness washed over me. I was suddenly no longer hungry myself.

In the past, when the men talked of war, I hadn't felt afraid. I had somehow known we would be spared.

This time, war would come to Kocho. I was sure of it because where my visions of the future were supposed to be, I now saw only a hole.

Chapter Three

August 3, 2014

The Stranger

I woke to the clanging of pots and pans. My mother and my sisters flitted back and forth from the bedroom to the kitchen, talking in hushed voices.

I pulled my arm, asleep and tingling, out from underneath Eivan. The night before, he had wanted to sleep with his father. But Fallah hadn't gone to bed. For the past few nights, he'd joined Adil on night patrols of our village. So instead, I had stroked Eivan's back as I told him the Yazidi creation story: For forty thousand years, there was great pain and suffering. God's seven angels were lost in a raging sea, but finally, they saw land. Lalish. The angels got off the boat and went ashore. Thus, the earth was formed. Once Eivan's eyes started to flutter, I sang him one of Adlan's lullabies until he fell asleep beside me.

Eivan's hair was tousled. I watched now as his chest rose and fell to the rhythm of his dreams. His mouth was wide open. "These dark days will pass, the sun will shine again," I sang softly the chorus of Adlan's lullaby.

I tiptoed to the kitchen, where my sisters were filling boxes with flour, cooking oils, nuts, rice, pears, apricots, and apples. Hassan and Fallah's voices rose and fell in the guest room.

"What's going on?" I asked.

"We're leaving," Majida said, looking worried.

"Khalil convinced Hassan to let us go to the mountains," Hadil explained as she put some tomatoes in a box. "Hassan will remain in Kocho along with Fallah and Adil to fight Daesh if they invade."

"We're like the Jews," I heard Fallah shouting as I took over for Adlan, putting plates, cups, and cutlery in another basket. We were packing items the way we did when we went to Lalish or on a picnic. "They were butchered in Germany, kicked out of Iraq . . . maybe we should have learned from them that these bad times were coming. We should never have been silent when Saddam moved the Arabs off their land in the south and into our area. We stood by and let Saddam take over our lands and suppress our culture."

Hassan yelled back that Fallah was being melodramatic. "Our Arab neighbors won't let Daesh hurt us."

I wasn't sure my father was right. I often read his newspapers when he was done with them and I knew that Daesh had grown out of al-Qaeda, the group that had attacked the World Trade Center in New York City in 2001. After the Americans declared war on Iraq, many al-Qaeda militants, or *jihadis,* were killed or imprisoned. Some regrouped in Syria, though, and they received money from wealthy Middle Eastern investors who wanted to see the leader of Syria, Bashar al-Assad, removed. The new group, Daesh, released the terrorists the Americans had imprisoned in Iraq and broke ties with al-Qaeda. Daesh wanted to create an Islamic state, which they called a caliphate. I wasn't sure what this Islamic state would mean for non-Muslims, like us, and it worried me.

I crept up behind my mother. "Could we pray?"

Adlan stopped what she was doing and stared at me in surprise. Usually, I prayed only when we were in Lalish. My mother seemed to have grown old since Daesh had taken over Mosul a few months earlier. Deep lines creased her eyes and mouth, making her look as if she were permanently frowning. The skin on her face drooped. Looking at her, I remembered something else she had told me. "Our fears are what age us," she had said. "Sickness starts in the mind and soul. Love makes us whole. Be fearless, Badeeah, in your giving and receiving of love.

Do not listen to a mind full of worry or hate. That kind of mind slowly kills you."

With her bony, arthritic hands, Adlan untied her apron. Just outside the living room hung a small package wrapped in white cloth made from trees found at Lalish. This package was what we called the Berat. Inside the cloth was soil that had been collected at the foot of the Shikefa Berata, or the Cave of Berat. The Shikefa Berata, we Yazidi believe, is from another planet. The cave is only opened once a year, when the energy inside has reached its peak. At this time, the earth in the cave is culled and placed in packages for each Yazidi family. The Berat is considered to have great healing properties.

I watched as my mother softly kissed the Berat. She stepped back and urged me to do the same. We Yazidi say that our Berat lets the angels know where to find us. My mother and I turned in the direction of the sun and said a prayer. "Amen. Amen. Amen," she concluded. "Blessed be our faith. God will help our faith survive."

My father's voice startled us. "I'm surprised to see you praying. Usually, it seems all you young people want to do is dance," he teased.

I pretended to glower at him. But what he said was in part true. Whenever there was dancing, I got to see Nafaa. I wanted so badly to tell Hassan and Adlan that the two of us were in love. Since I was the youngest girl in the family, my parents, I knew, would want me to hold off until I was in my mid-twenties before thinking about marriage since Adlan would need me around the home to help with the farming and the chores. But maybe if I told them about Nafaa, my visions of my future with him would appear again. I opened my mouth, then closed it quickly as Eivan cried out. Adlan turned back to the kitchen. I followed.

Eivan was by now playing on the floor with his yellow-and-white toy taxi. "Naan," he said when he saw me. I whisked him into my arms and then high into the air, spinning him around the room.

He shouted, his laughter flying around him. Hassan started clapping out the beats to the old traditional Kurdish song "Shamame." By the time he was done, both Eivan and I were panting. But Eivan didn't want to stop.

Adlan winked at me and handed me some flatbread. "We'll leave for the mountains in an hour or so. Go outside and play until we're ready."

Eivan and I made our way toward the primary school, kicking a worn football between us as we nibbled our breakfast. It was Fallah's football from when he was a child. It had a tear, which make it slow and zigzaggy, and Eivan liked that part best of all. He ran after the ball, twisting along with it. His laugh bounced off the clay houses we passed. Most of them were similar to ours: rectangular, with a guest room in the front for men and male visitors, a living room where family hung out, a kitchen, and a bedroom in the back. There were separate buildings beside or behind the houses that we used as outhouses. Some of the homes had second stories. Pipes brought in water, which each household collected in buckets from the outside faucets. We had electricity, but it went off regularly. Each house had a generator for those days when the power was off for long periods of time. In our kitchen, we had a gas stove and a refrigerator. Our generator was never powerful enough to chill the freezer.

Adlan said we shouldn't complain that we didn't have hot water or twenty-four-hour electricity. Saddam's cousin, Ali Hassan al-Majid, had killed entire villages of Kurds during the al-Anfal campaign, a genocide from 1986 to 1989. Under Saddam's rule, many Yazidi villages had been taken over by Arabs and the residents sent to displaced people's camps. Adlan said Kocho was safe because of the Arab men in nearby villages who were Kirivs to Yazidi boys. When a Yazidi boy is circumcised, his Kiriv places him on his lap, indicating that he promises to watch over and guide him for his whole life. Yazidi families accepted their sons' Kirivs as brothers. Because the Yazidi only marry other Yazidi, families often chose Muslim Kirivs to unite the religions.

"The men talk too much," Eivan said, as if reading my thoughts. Adlan said that Eivan was like Fallah when he was little: inquisitive, sharp, and hearing things when others thought he wasn't listening. Eivan's irises sparkled and his long lashes glistened, as if he had just passed through a cloud. Looking at him, warmth moved through me and I began to relax, telling myself that the anxiety I had felt the night before was just my mind playing a trick on me. Eivan and I kicked the ball back and forth some more.

But on our way home, as we passed the Jevata Gundi, where the men held their political meetings, the hairs on the back of my neck stood on end. The street was usually full of women heading to the farms or the shops, men sitting outside talking politics, and children playing sneak-and-hide, along with pigeons, donkeys, dogs, baaing sheep, and squawking chickens. That day, though, Kocho was a ghost town.

Eivan reached over and gripped my hand tight. I stopped cold, yanking him behind a house under construction. We hid underneath some wooden scaffolding draped with white plastic sheeting. My hand covered his mouth.

"Be quiet," I whispered into his ear.

Ever so slowly, I poked my head out.

A group of men had gathered outside the Jevata Gundi. Ahmed Jasso, our mukhtar, was among them. Beside him was a tall man I'd never seen before, wearing a caramel-colored dishdasha. My brothers Adil and Fallah were standing off to the side, fingering the leather straps on the rifles slung over their backs. They stood with their legs spread, their chests puffed out, their chins high.

"You'll be safe," Ahmed Jasso assured the group of men. "We've come to an agreement with the Islamic

State. They won't attack our village. But you have to give up your weapons." He gestured for the men of Kocho to follow him into the building, where he said they could talk some more.

As the village men filed in, including my brothers, the man in the dishdasha hung back. "Hand over your weapons or the peace agreement with the Islamic State will be broken," he shouted as he followed the last Kocho man into the building. "Kocho will be attacked in less than twenty-four hours if you don't."

My stomach clenched. Eivan squirmed, and I realized my hand was still covering his mouth.

I had just let go of Eivan when two men passed in front of our hiding place. I jumped instinctively, my back coming up flush against a newly built wall. The men were not from Kocho. They were dressed in black, with large belts of ammunition stretched across their stomachs. They were holding rifles, long semiautomatic weapons like Hassan's.

"These Yazidi are *abadat shaytan*," I heard one say in Arabic. He was calling us devil worshippers. I was fluent in the language after six years of study.

"These non-believers, if they don't convert, they're sabaya," the other said. "War booty." He laughed, revealing yellow teeth and black gums.

Those words again: *sabaya. War booty.* I didn't know quite what they meant, but I was sure it would not be a good thing for us Yazidi.

∾

Hearing the two men in black brought back a strong memory. On one of our family trips to Lalish, Hassan had driven a different way. Near Mosul, he slowed to show us the oil refineries: tall sticks blowing out thick smoke, mountain-sized buildings, masses of twinkling lights, and machines that sparkled in the sun.

"It's oil that causes war," my father said in a barely audible voice. "You'll hear that Saddam doesn't like us because we're 'abadat shaytan' and followers of Iblis, the devil. But greed is the root of his hatred."

At the mention of abadat shaytan, my mother gasped. I was sitting beside her in the back seat and she gripped my hand.

"What is abadat shaytan?" I whispered.

Adlan shook her head. "Don't speak those words," she scolded. "Zoroastrians said the devil made a peacock to show his powers. But we believe the peacock represents Tawsi Malak, the angel we look to as an example. Another reason the Yazidi have been persecuted is because our spirituality is so old. When conquerors came to our area and learned of our powers, they assumed we were playing with dark forces. That's why we Yazidi don't share our wisdom now with the rest of the world. And then there is the Quran," she continued. "The devil is described in it as an angel who refused God's order to bow down before Adam. Tawsi Malak didn't pray to Adam, so some Muslims say that he is the devil."

"Is he?" I asked.

"No," she said. "Tawsi Malak was one of seven angels, or *malayika*. God gave each of them a special gift. On Tawsi Malak God bestowed light and inner sight. God then told the angels to make humankind. The angels made Adam. God asked the angels to bow to Adam and Tawsi Malak was the only angel who refused, saying that he had made a promise never to bow to anyone but God. We Yazidi revere Tawsi Malak for his faithfulness to the only source of power in this world, God."

Hassan turned to my brother Fallah and said, "They say we have no religion because we have no book like the Jewish Torah, the Quran, the Hindu Vedas, or the Christian Bible. They say the Yazidi aren't a real culture. But those are lies." My father paused. "The real reason the Yazidi are not wanted here is power. Our land is rich in oil."

Adlan bit her lip to keep it from trembling. "Greed and anger," she said in a shaky voice. "A door in our mind allows these monsters to enter. In this country, Badeeah, the door of greed is opened wide."

∽

Eighteen of us squeezed ourselves into Khalil's pickup truck.

I sat in the corner of the cargo bed, right up close to the driver, with Eivan on my lap, surrounded by ten of my cousins.

As Khalil drove, he talked loudly in the front seat about the tall man negotiating with Ahmed Jasso. Apparently, the man in the dishdasha was named Abu Hamza. He was Muslim but not a friend, Khalil said. Abu Hamza was a common thug. Hussain, a man from our village, had been in prison in Mosul with Abu Hamza before Daesh freed many of the prisoners, encouraging them to join Daesh's ranks.

Khalil said that Ahmed Jasso and some of the other Kocho elders trusted Abu Hamza, but he didn't think they should. The Peshmerga, the Kurdish military force, had recently left Kocho, claiming they had to ward off Daesh advances in Tal Banat. But that was also gossip being taken as truth, he said. He was now shouting to be heard over the clanging of the truck on the bumpy road. "The Peshmerga in all the Yazidi towns and in Shingal have just retreated. It is like they were ordered to withdraw." The other forces in the area, including the border guards and the Iraqi army, which had been patrolling the roads into Shingal, had also disappeared. "We don't even have our weapons anymore to defend ourselves," he cried.

I'd brought along Eivan's football, hoping we'd have some time to play in the countryside. Listening anxiously to Khalil, I began weaving the material that had come loose back into the seam of the football.

As we neared the road to the mountain, the truck slowed.

Cars and trucks from other Yazidi villages were vying for spots on the road. Car after car, truck after truck, were piled high like ours, with bedding, boxes, bags, suitcases, and people. It was hot, a stifling heat, so everybody's windows were down. People called out to one another. Men shared cigarettes, talked politics, and passed on news of what they had heard and seen. Women asked after each other's families, hoping everyone was safe.

For about a mile, Khalil's truck moved at a crawl.

Then, as we got to the road that led up the mountain, the traffic stopped moving.

Khalil honked his horn, swore, and pounded his fists on the dashboard. Eivan fidgeted in my arms. "He is scared," he said.

"No, he's just angry," I assured him. The little boy tucked his head into my neck.

For as far as we could see, there were vehicles, a parade of Yazidi residents trying to escape.

Adlan asked Khalil to turn on some music, but Kurdish news came on the radio instead. The newscaster was talking about Daesh moving into Shingal.

Khalil's phone rang. "What is it?" he spat into the receiver. Everyone was on edge. Through the tiny window in the cargo bed, I could see Fallah's temples throbbing.

The Nokia phones we used were cheap, and the acoustics were terrible. I could hear the person on the other end as if he were in the truck with us. It was my father, saying that Ahmed Jasso had made an agreement with Daesh. If the Yazidi converted to Islam, we could stay in Kocho. If we didn't, Daesh would move us to Kurdistan. Either way, they didn't want to hurt us. Ahmed Jasso had bought us some time, I heard my father explaining, by saying he needed a few days to ask people if they wanted to convert. Our mukhtar's request was actually a ruse to give everyone time to pack up their belongings. Hassan wanted us home so we could do that together.

It was dark by the time we were able to turn the truck around and start heading back to Kocho.

Khalil no longer spoke. Silence cut into us all like a knife as we brooded on the latest developments. I knew from Adlan's history lessons that the Yazidi people had been pressured to convert to Islam since the thirteenth century. Many did because the alternative was death. Adlan would be sad to leave Kocho, where she had built up a life for herself. But Hassan had been talking to my brothers about moving anyway, building a second home in Shingal to be closer to his work.

My initial shock soon turned to optimism. In Kurdistan, there would be schools with a secular curriculum. I could look into finishing high school and then study nursing or medicine at a college. I imagined Nafaa, who had been selling chocolates and other sweets since finishing primary school. In Kurdistan, he could study to be a lawyer, which was his dream. In a few years, I would tell Adlan and Hassan about us. Maybe Nafaa and I would never leave Kurdistan, building a home there. These thoughts made me feel so upbeat that, at first, I didn't notice the truck slowing.

Then I looked over at Adlan's face, which was pinched.

We were passing through the Yazidi village of Tel Qasab, about fifteen minutes from Kocho. Darkness cloaked us. The village was black. Not a single light from any of the houses.

Then I spied dancing lights from torches approaching our truck. A roadblock. Nothing new. There were checkpoints everywhere in Iraq, usually armed by Iraqi or Peshmerga soldiers asking to see ID and checking to make sure vehicles weren't carrying weapons or terrorists.

This time, though, my heart began to thump. The men guarding the roadblock weren't dressed in the Iraqi army uniform or in the Peshmerga green and khaki. They were in black.

Fallah cursed.

Adlan took Eivan from me and held him tight. My mouth went dry.

Two Daesh soldiers walked up to the driver's side and pointed their weapons into the car. One waved his AK-47 at Khalil, shouting at him to get out.

Khalil's door creaked open. I held my breath as my uncle raised his shaking hands and stepped outside.

Standing behind the two Daesh soldiers was a group of men dressed in dishdashas. They were the ones carrying the torches. As they inched their way forward, I heard one call out, "Khalil? Khalil Ahmed from Kocho?"

Khalil's face had turned white.

"Khalil from Kocho?" I heard the voice call again. A smiling older man stepped in front of my uncle and said something to the Daesh men holding the weapons.

"It's Abu Anwar," muttered my cousin Brahim, who was sitting close to me. "He's my Kiriv."

I could hear my mother exhale. Like me, she had been holding her breath.

Abu Anwar and the other Arab men moved in to surround Khalil. They talked for a while in muffled voices, and then Khalil gestured for Brahim to join him. The rest of us sat in the truck swatting away the night flies.

Finally, Khalil and Brahim returned, climbing silently into the truck. With my uncle behind the wheel again, we drove slowly through the checkpoint. We were nearly in Kocho before they explained what had happened. Abu Anwar, Brahim's Kiriv, had told Daesh that our two families were close. We were allowed to return home, but Abu Anwar had warned my uncle that we were not to leave Kocho on our own again. The next time, he might not be there to secure our safety.

Chapter Four

August 15, 2014

Invasion

The walls of our house shook.

Trucks roared down the road. Some were sparkling white, with missile launchers in the cargo beds. Some were armored trucks with long gun barrels.

I ran.

Suddenly, I wasn't in Kocho anymore but in a thick forest of Zagros oak trees. I seemed to be in the hills near the Turkish border. A man was chasing me, calling out in a language I recognized from BBC news reports as English.

Then it was no longer day. The only light came from a half-moon behind a thin veil of clouds. I tripped *and fell, hitting my head on a rock. My head throbbed with pain, but I scrambled to get up. The man was approaching fast.*

I called out for help, but all that came back to me was my own voice bouncing off the rocks.

Soon I was running again, until I spotted Eivan. He was slumped beside a stream, as if leaning into the water to play. I was so happy to see him. But as I neared, I realized that he wasn't playing at all but was asleep, with one hand in the stream. The other was twisted behind his back, as if it was broken. I screamed.

I woke from the nightmare, panting. After I steadied myself, I looked around. The gray light of dawn was meandering its way between the window and the curtains in the bedroom. I could hear the familiar sounds of morning: nightingales singing, pigeons cooing, and chickens squabbling. I breathed in the scent of camphor oil, cinnamon, nutmeg, and allspice—spices used so often by my mother in her recipes that they had become one with our house, along with the bitter incense from Lalish that she burned every Tuesday evening. The Yazidi consider sunset to be the start of the day so Tuesday evening is actually Wednesday morning. Wednesday is our rest day. We believe it is the day the world was made.

Since our return on the night of August 3, I'd barely left the house. The farthest I dared go was the outhouse or the garden, where Eivan and I kicked the football back and forth and played sneak-and-hide. Even though I hadn't seen them, I knew Daesh had come to our village with Abu Hamza as he negotiated our move to Kurdistan with Ahmed Jasso. I knew through listening to the men's conversations that Yazidi were flocking to Kocho from other villages and from Shingal, trying to escape Daesh. Daesh was also directing Yazidi from other towns and even Shingal to Kocho.

There was no electricity at all now, and we used the generator sparingly. The nights were long and dark, with the Yazidi men staying up to guard the house, do patrols, and argue about what to do next. Adlan and my sisters rarely talked. Like me, they didn't go out. The house filled with our fear and tension as we waited.

I pulled on a dress and a pair of pants, ran a brush through my hair, and grabbed an off-white sweater I had knit with my grandmother's help just before she died. I opened the door slowly, making sure not to wake Majida and Hadil. Their long, dark hair was spread out across their sleeping mats. Their blankets and sheets were wound tightly around them, as if they, too, had had fitful dreams.

I moved to the hallway to pray but stopped dead in my tracks. The Berat was missing.

I cried out for my mother to come.

"What happened?" she stammered, kneeling in front of me.

"Where is the Berat?" I asked, pointing a trembling finger at the empty space where it had been.

"Hassan scattered the soil outside," Adlan said, sitting down on the floor beside me. Terror gripped me as my mother explained that Daesh wanted our money, jewelry, and homes.

When Yazidi people moved houses, we always left the Berat behind. As was customary, it didn't travel with us. At the same time, if a house was destroyed or burned down with the Berat inside, it was considered a terrible spiritual blow. That my father had scattered the soil meant he feared the worst was coming.

"He prayed at the same time for God to protect us and our land," my mother was saying. "He says Daesh are thieves, not freedom fighters."

"But I thought he said there was nothing to worry about."

Adlan looked away. "Badeeah, give me your earrings," she said, her voice barely a murmur. With shaking hands, I unclipped the gold earrings my father had given me when I was twelve, stars attached to three dangling pillars. They were the only jewelry I owned.

"I've been having such bad dreams," I confessed as I handed her the earrings. I watched as she wrapped them in some tissue and tucked them into her orange belt. I could see wads of dinar tied with an elastic band, and

I noticed that Adlan had put her gold earrings and necklaces there, too.

She tried to hide it but I could see that my mother was crying. Tears dripped down her cheeks.

"We are all having bad dreams," she said.

We spent the morning continuing to pack for our move to Kurdistan. I was folding some sheets when Adlan called for me to turn the generator on. "We need some air conditioning," she yelled.

It was smoldering outside, a dry heat that charred anything left out in it for too long. As I slipped on my shoes, Khudher rushed up beside me, offering to help. "It needs gas," Adlan called as Khudher and I stepped out the front door.

The generator was tucked in around the back of our house, near the outhouse.

When we reached the generator, I bent over to hold the funnel so Khudher could pour the gas.

As he lit the match to start the generator, a fiery blue, yellow, and green cloud leapt out at me, biting into my leg. I fell back screaming as pain shot through me. I looked down and saw that a hole had been burned through my dress and pant leg.

Where the fire had singed my leg, the skin was red and already bubbling. Crying with pain, I fled back into the house, where Adlan helped me change into another dress and then put yogurt on my skin to cool the burn. To calm me, she sang a lullaby. But my crying didn't stop.

Shaking, I reached out and grabbed Adlan and Khudher by their arms. The accident was a bad omen. I just knew it. "Something terrible is going to happen," I choked out. "I'm so scared."

Seconds later, our house began to shake, just like in my nightmare. Adlan's metal pots and tea glasses clanked. Hot air and dust blew in through the open windows. My mother tossed me a pair of brown cotton pants to put on.

In the other room, I could hear Eivan starting to cry.

I limped to the front window behind Khudher, only to step back in shock. White trucks, some with missile launchers in the cargo beds, rumbled past our house, followed by huge army tanks.

When I felt Eivan tugging at the hem of my dress, I looked down. In his other hand, he clutched his toy taxi. "Can I see?" he begged. He was too short to look out the window himself. But I couldn't move to lift him. I stood frozen as one after the other, the white trucks zoomed past, carrying men dressed head to toe in black.

Finally, the roar of the vehicles dimmed.

As the dust settled, a hush fell over us.

"They're gone," I said.

Eivan's eyes darted back and forth, and he made puffing sounds like when he was pretending to be a monster. But this time, he wasn't pretending. "We have to hide," he whimpered. "Baba told me, when they came, we should hide."

"Hide where?"

"In the outhouse!"

"But ... we're safe," I stammered. "We're just going to Kurdistan." I could speak, but my body still felt stuck.

"Baba said it would be like sneak-and-hide." Eivan reached out and took my hand. "Come with me. We need to get nuts and fruit," he said, pulling me. "Small things that will fit in our pockets ..."

Paralyzed by fear, I watched Eivan head on his wobbly legs to the kitchen. "Baba says wear an extra layer of clothes because the nights are cold," he called back over his shoulder.

Hadil, Khudher, Majida, and Adlan had rolled up our bedding and were loading the car with our supplies. They seemed calm. Maybe they viewed the trucks as a sign we were finally moving to Kurdistan.

A phone rang.

I jumped.

Adlan answered. It was my brother Adil saying that Daesh wanted everybody in our village to come to the middle school. We were supposed to bring all of our things, including our money and our jewels. It was time. We were leaving Kocho.

Eivan, back from the kitchen with his pockets bulging with food, slipped his sweaty palm into mine. "We should hide," he insisted. Adil flew in through the front door, yelling at us to hurry up. Both Hassan's used BMW, which he had bought when he was elected into politics, and Adil's car were idling outside.

A part of me left my body then. I was back in my nightmare. The white trucks storming the village. The forest of Zagros oak trees. Eivan sliding into the water. As my dream flashed across my mind, I knew Eivan was right. We had to hide.

"Let's go!" I turned to find him.

But he wasn't there.

My sister Majida had him. Eivan was flailing around as she carried him out the door. He stretched his arms out toward me. But Majida wouldn't let him go.

I grabbed my sweater and shoes and headed outside.

Majida was putting Eivan into the back seat of Adil's car.

"Majida," I yelled, as she crouched beside him. "Majida, I need to take Eivan."

"What for?" she snapped.

"I don't trust Daesh," I said, stuttering. "We need to hide."

"No." She slammed the car door shut.

Eivan glared at me from the other side of the car window, angry I hadn't listened to him. I hopped from foot to foot putting on my shoes. The burn on my leg pulsed with pain, but there was no time to think about it.

Reluctantly, I climbed into the back of Hassan's BMW with my mother and Hadil. I could see our neighbors getting into their vehicles, too. As we waited for our father, who was still loading up the car, Hadil jabbered that everything was okay, that the soldiers didn't want to harm us. "We've done this before, Adlan, remember?" she said. "Remember?"

I could feel Adlan's back stiffen. Hadil had a bad habit of always saying the wrong thing. She was referring to the time the Iraqi army had taken Fallah. Our father had held my mother's arms behind her back as she tried to run after the truck with her son inside it. For nearly a month after that, my sisters and I did all the cooking and the planting at the farm because Adlan wouldn't get out of bed. Hassan told us her heart was broken.

I wished Hadil would be quiet.

"We're going to Kurdistan to start a new life," she prattled on.

My mother fidgeted with her hair. As always, strands were falling out of her kufi. I reached over to help. Adlan, I knew, wanted to make herself presentable. Even if the men who had come to our village were enemies, she would greet them the Yazidi way: politely. "Bring in the stranger and they become your brother or sister," she would always say.

As Hassan drove, I looked around the village. Almost everyone had already left to meet Daesh. I realized with a jolt that I couldn't see or hear any animals: no chickens, goats, or donkeys . . . even the dogs in the village seemed to be gone.

And birdsong. There was none.

A shiver ran through me as I remembered a television program I had seen when I was a child. At the time, Hassan had just been elected as the representative for the Kurdistan Democratic Party. He had used his first paycheck to buy a color TV from the secondhand market in Mosul. I liked the moving images on the screen and would sneak into the living room to watch TV when no one else was around. The world came to me that way: places and people and especially the oceans, which I had never seen because we lived in the middle of the desert. The colors of the water came alive for me—lapis lazuli blues, glimmering emerald greens. I imagined what it would be like to travel by boat and see the Rockies of North America, the sprawling cities of Europe, and the beaches of the Far East. One program I caught was about a tsunami that had hit India and parts of the Middle East in 2004. The Kurdish narrator talked about how birds and animals have a built-in sense that tells them danger is imminent. Before the tsunami, many dogs, cats, and birds escaped to higher ground, as if their radar had given them advance warning.

I watched Eivan's head bobbing up and down in the back seat of Adil's car directly in front of us. Guilt moved through me in waves. I should have listened to Eivan. The two of us should have run away.

Chapter Five

Sabaya

Daesh's white pickup trucks and armored tanks circled the school. Daesh men lumbered back and forth, many of them wearing black clothes with ammunition draped around their torsos. A wave of dizziness washed over me as I watched them. My burned leg throbbed. I gritted my teeth and linked my arm through my mother's.

A Daesh man marched over to the BMW and motioned for us to park, instructing my father to leave the keys in the ignition. "Bring your money, jewelry, and cell phones with you," the Daesh man snarled.

When we got out of the vehicle, Hassan was shoved toward a line of men. Adlan and I merged with the women and children, losing sight of Hadil, Majida, and Eivan in the crowd.

As we neared the entrance to the school, Daesh men forced us to halt in front of some blankets that had been stretched out on the ground. On one were piles of coins and wads of dinar. On another were cell phones. And on another were necklaces and bracelets made of gold and silver, some inlaid with diamonds and other gemstones. Kocho was wealthy because we had so much land on which to plant and harvest our crops. Tucked in between Syria and the rest of Iraq, we also had many markets where we could sell our goods.

A lump rose in my throat as I looked down at our village's riches. A Daesh soldier punched Adlan in the shoulder with the barrel of his gun. "Give it over," he hissed in Arabic, pointing at her belt. It was clear Daesh knew the women's hiding places. Beads of perspiration dotted my mother's upper lip. The soldier snapped at her again, and Adlan's crooked fingers slipped underneath her belt. I watched her withdraw the dinar first, then my earrings, and finally, with a trembling hand, her gold jewelry, some of which was from her wedding to my father.

Inside the school building, Adlan and I climbed the stairs to the second floor, my nails digging into her flesh. That was in part so I wouldn't lose her and in part from nerves. We moved with the current of other Yazidi girls and women until we found ourselves in a classroom. The classroom reminded me of the one in primary school where I had taken some of my grades. During break time there, I would play house with my cousin Nadia. We each had fabric dolls sewn by our mothers. Our dolls were dressed in Yazidi costumes—white dresses with red belts, to symbolize love, and kufis on their heads.

Now the room was filled with women and girls shaking with fear and holding each other tight.

Above us on the third floor, we could hear the heavy footsteps of Daesh men, their haunting laughs and their loud Arabic conversations.

No one in the classroom spoke. Suddenly, the door slammed shut and the windows shook.

A black cloud enveloped us. Night seemed to have fallen outside, despite it being midday.

Women started to scream. Children cried out in terror. Someone shouted that it was the end of the world.

Adlan and I, folded into each other's arms, looked out the window in stunned silence. It was a sandstorm. Sand had whipped up, circling faster and faster, blinding us to everything outside.

Doors opened and banged shut as wind howled through the hallways of the school. Suddenly, I couldn't swallow or breathe.

I squeezed my eyes shut.

∾

Finally, the sandstorm ended and daylight returned. But those of us trapped inside the room were still gripped in a nightmare.

Above and around us, we heard scuffling, then gunshots. A shock ran through the room as we grasped each other. Old women mumbled their prayers.

Ahmed Jasso, our mukhtar, came into the classroom, his face strained and red. Perspiration stained the armpits of his shirt. In a quivering voice, he said that if we had held back any dinar, phones, or jewelry, we must hand it over now. "Let's just pay Daesh off and get out of the village," he implored, reminding us that Daesh had promised to take us to Kurdistan. From behind Ahmed Jasso emerged a tall, fat man in a long, brown dishdasha with a black scarf worn loosely over his head.

Sanaa, a girl I knew from my primary school, gripped my free arm. A woman I didn't recognize and her four children crowded in close behind me.

"Are you going to convert to Islam?" the fat man shouted. His booming voice bounced off the walls. The classroom was empty except for our bodies. The school had recently sold all its desks and chairs and was waiting for new ones to be delivered.

The man was so huge he reminded me of an oak tree. He had even had to duck as he came through the door. I looked quickly at his face and then away, but not before I saw his eyes. They were dark and cold, like shiny black marbles.

"Where are you from?" the woman with the four children called to him.

The man tilted his head and studied the woman. A chill ran through me. I was afraid for the woman, but she was not intimidated. She stepped toward the man, her children still attached to her. "I'm a doctor in Shingal," she said. "I'm in Kocho with my children. You need to let us go."

"Are you converting to Islam?" the man spat out, taking a giant step toward her. His spittle landed on the woman's face.

To my surprise, my mother spoke up. In a meek voice, she asked our mukhtar, "How did our men answer?"

"They refused," Ahmed Jasso said.

One after another, the women in the room lowered their heads and mumbled that they wouldn't convert—everyone except the doctor from Shingal. She moved up close to the man in the dishdasha. "You need to release us," she said again, her voice full of authority. "All of us."

"What's your name?" the man asked.

"Manje," she said. "And yours? Where are you from? Saudi Arabia? I can tell by your Arabic."

The man scratched his beard, which, like his hair, was black, curly, and coarse. Then he snickered. "Are you converting to Islam?" he asked Manje again.

Manje shook her head slowly. The fat man snapped his fingers, and three Daesh, dressed in black and wearing face coverings, rushed into the room. One of them grabbed Manje. Her children shrieked as their mother was torn away from them. The second man pointed his rifle at the rest of us. The third held a long knife like the kind used to slaughter animals. As Manje was dragged from the room by the collar of her dress, her children tried to run after her. Other women in the room held onto them as they struggled to get free.

The man with the knife sneered at us to get moving downstairs to the courtyard. The women and children in the room started screaming then, so loudly my eardrums rang.

I held on tight to my mother's hand, but as we neared the final step, I felt her hand being pried away from mine. Someone had grabbed hold of one of my arms and was twisting it. Fleshy hands pushed me out into the crowd. When I finally managed to turn around, Adlan had disappeared.

Tears streamed down my cheeks. "Mama!" I yelled.

I was caught up in a sea of bodies; all the women and girls and some small boys.

Where were our men?

Ahead of me, I could see a group of girls, including my cousin Nadia and my sisters Hadil and Majida. They were getting into the cargo bed of one of our farm trucks as Daesh men with guns stood by. Ahmed Jasso called out for us to settle down. "We're going to Solakh," he shouted, referring to one of the many Yazidi villages surrounding Shingal. "From there, you will be reunited with the men and we'll head to Kurdistan." As he spoke, he flapped his hand, indicating that we should be quiet and calm down. But his clenched teeth and furrowed forehead belied his words.

Just then, twelve-year-old Aryan, the son of a man named Ali, pushed his way past me. Aryan's face was red, slathered in snot and tears. He was yelling that Daesh had killed his father. "I saw, I saw," he screamed, drowning out Ahmed Jasso, who was continuing to plead with us not to worry. "Daesh are murderers!" Ali said.

I strained my eyes to find my brothers and Hassan. The sound of gunshots bounced against the cement. More screaming.

My head spun, my legs weakened, and I found myself sinking toward the ground. As my body slumped forward, I saw it.

Eivan's taxi was buried in some sand. I grabbed it quickly and tucked it into the pocket of my sweater.

"Eivan!" I yelled, knowing he had to be near. "Eivan!"

A thump on my back. Hands pulling me up by my clothing. A fist in the base of my spine pushing me forward. A Daesh soldier was shoving me and shouting at me to go with the other young women.

I spied the huge Saudi Arabian man from the classroom in front of me. He was standing with his legs spread and his arms folded across his wide chest. His eyes were focused on something behind me. I turned to follow his gaze and saw that he was looking at Eivan.

I took a deep breath, dug my heels into the ground, and ducked down low, out from underneath the Daesh man behind me. I darted toward Eivan and whisked him into my arms seconds before the Saudi Arabian man reached him.

Eivan was trembling and calling out for his father. I put my lips up close to his ear and told him to shush. But he wouldn't.

"Who is that?" the Saudi man demanded, pointing at Eivan.

My mind churned.

Eivan was sobbing now. I wanted him to stop so I could think. I spied Viyan, a new mother, getting into the back seat of another one of our trucks. In her arms was her baby.

"Who is that?" the man said again, stepping in so close I could feel his steamy breath on my cheek.

"My son," I said breathlessly. "My son," I repeated in a louder voice.

I looked down, not wanting my eyes to give away my lie.

I watched the man clench and unclench his fists. His knuckles were hairy and big like the rest of him, and they bulged white against his brown skin. His fingernails were dirty, as if he'd been digging in dirt.

I rocked Eivan back and forth. "Shush," I cooed into his ear.

"Over there," the man eventually grunted, pointing toward the truck carrying Viyan and her baby.

As I walked, I caught glimpses of Arab men from nearby towns. They were standing off to the side, staring, doing nothing to stop Daesh. I recognized many men, men who would drop by the house for tea with Hassan. Brahim's Kiriv Abu Anwar was there, in the middle of the group. When our eyes met, he quickly looked away.

I had no time to think with Eivan still crying and calling out for his father.

Terror moved through me. What if he asked for his real mother next and my deceit was revealed? I needed Eivan to settle down and trust me.

I moved my mouth up so that my lips touched his ear. I whispered to him about the time I'd been lost in the forest near Lalish and a butterfly rose out of the mist to guide me back to the others.

"Has your mother told you about Khatuna Fakhra yet?" I asked, speaking as low as I could. Eivan murmured no.

"For everything in the universe, there is an opposite. Khatuna Fakhra represents the energy of women. She is the feminine of the universe, the female part of our culture. She is an angel, a legend, a holy person. Her energy guides and protects women and girls and children. Think of her now. Like the butterfly who guided me in Lalish, she will bring you safely home again," I told Eivan as we shifted in beside Viyan.

Thankfully, he quieted at my words.

∽

Once we were in the truck, I held Eivan on my lap with his face turned inward so he couldn't see what was happening. Beside me sat Viyan and her baby. On the other side of her a woman named Ghalya held her baby close.

The cries of women and children amplified as more gunshots rang out, this time rapid-fire from automatic rifles followed by single shots.

Eivan's body turned hard and cold.

"What's going on?" Viyan shouted at the Daesh soldier who had hopped into the driver's seat. He wasn't wearing a face scarf, and I shifted so I could see him in the rearview mirror. He looked younger than me.

Another round of gunshots rang out.

When the soldier turned to face us, I could see that I'd been right. Our driver was just a child, barely a teenager. "We're killing your dogs," he said, his lip curling into a snarl.

"You're not killing our dogs," I returned, startling myself by speaking up. Anger bubbled inside of me, anger at what war did to children, what it had done to my brothers Adil and Fallah, and what it was now doing to this boy, who had become one of the enemy. The driver glared at me. "All the dogs have left," I pressed on. "They ran away when you came."

The boy made as if to punch me. I squeezed my eyes shut. When I opened them again, he was fumbling with the keys in the ignition. He didn't even know how to turn the truck on. Finally, he got the key in properly. The engine backfired and the vehicle rocked on its wheels. Soon we began to creep through town, past Kocho's shops and the dirt roads and paths that led to our farms, and then past our houses.

I locked my eyes tight onto my family's front door until eventually it faded from view.

Chapter Six

Prisoner

A convoy had left Kocho, with Daesh driving us in our own vehicles. The rumble of car and truck engines was deafening at first.

As we drove, I rocked Eivan in my arms and thought about my mother and all she had taught me about the Yazidi. "We are a strong people," she would say. "We've faced and survived seventy-two genocides. Do not hate, Badeeah. This is the test of survival, to not lose one's soul."

Our truck came to a stop.

I looked up and could see that we were in Hatimiya, the village near the special hill where we Yazidi bury our dead. The convoy seemed to have left us behind.

"What's happened?" Ghalya demanded. "Why are we stopping here?"

"I don't know where we are," the boy driver admitted, squeezing his fists tight around the steering wheel.

"What? Where are you from?" Viyan asked him.

"Mosul." The boy's voice was high-pitched.

I jumped in. "Where are we going?" I demanded.

"To Solakh to meet the others," he replied curtly. "Just like your mukhtar said."

"And then on to Kurdistan?" My voice quivered.

He nodded. I didn't believe him, but I had to hang onto something, even if it was just a sliver of hope.

"For real?" Ghalya chimed in.

"Yes!" he shouted. "But if I don't get you to Solakh, they'll kill us. All of us!"

Viyan, Ghalya, and I looked at each other, not sure what we should do.

The child soldier glanced at us and then away, as if he had been taught not to look us in the eye. "We don't want to hurt anyone," he said in a shaky voice.

"Why did they separate the men from the women?" I asked. "Why couldn't you just have taken us straight to Kurdistan?"

"We were afraid your men would rise up against us," the driver said. "Separated from you, we knew they wouldn't try to overpower us. In Solakh, we have reinforcements should your men decide to fight back."

"What about the gunshots?" I persisted. "Tell us the truth. You know the soldiers weren't killing our dogs."

"They were just bullets shot into the air," he said. Suddenly, I heard Aryan's voice in my head, shouting that his father, Ali, had been killed. My head pounded. My temples throbbed. I didn't know what to believe. I wanted this nightmare to be over.

Ghalya leaned forward and directed the boy out of the village and onto the road to Shingal and Solakh.

It was sunny again by now. The sandstorm was long gone, which puzzled me. In May and June, with the temperature and air pressure changing so fast, we expected sandstorms. Those storms didn't come from out of nowhere and then vanish, however. Not like the storm had today. Dark clouds usually came first, heralding the storm in their wake. Whatever had happened back in Kocho was rare, like a flash of lightning on a cloudless day.

Eivan groggily asked if we were going home.

"No. I think we're going to Kurdistan, where we will meet your mother and father," I said softly in his ear. "But Eivan, you must do something for me."

"What?"

"Call me Mama ... just until we reach Kurdistan, okay?"

"Why?" He looked up, rubbing his sleepy eyes with dusty fists.

"Because we're playing a game," I said, thinking fast.

Eivan's eyes lit up. He loved games.

"You know that butterfly I told you about? The one that led me out of the forest and back to Lalish?"

"Uh-huh?"

"There will be other things like the butterfly that will appear to help us. But they can only show themselves when we are still. If our heads are full of worry or we're upset or angry, these special forces will remain hidden. The first thing to do in the game is to call me Mama. If you're asked by anyone, you need to tell them I'm your mother. That's part of the game."

Eivan's lips parted in a weak smile.

"Put your hand in my pocket," I said.

When Eivan discovered his toy taxi, his eyes danced.

The young driver stopped the truck in front of the technical college in Solakh. My legs, cramped from sitting in the same position for so long, were stiff as I exited the vehicle. Any softness the driver had shown us disappeared as he acted tough in front of the other Daesh men. He shouted at me to hurry up, then kicked me in the back of the legs when I moved too slowly.

I winced, reminded again of my burned leg as I hoisted Eivan into my arms.

Once inside the building, Daesh soldiers herded us out back into the garden, where the other women and girls from our village had already gathered. Everyone wore the same expression of fear.

"What is going on?" I asked out loud.

"I don't know," I heard a familiar voice behind me say.

Tingling all over, I turned slowly. Adlan scurried up beside me and grasped my elbow.

Something had changed about her, I noticed. Her shoulders no longer slumped. Her eyes were not lined in dark circles. Color had returned to her face. Even her grasp was strong. A knowing rushed through me: my mother was no longer afraid.

She gathered Eivan into her arms, and we huddled in close to each other as we scanned the garden, looking for my sisters. Cement stones drew twisting paths through tall, willowy Spindar trees and short, fat evergreens that, on any other day, I would have loved to sit near and read a book. The grass was its typical August brown.

Adlan waved, and I looked up to see Hadil and Majida moving through the crowd toward us.

Behind my sisters walked a Daesh soldier handing out candies to the children. I shuddered as I recognized the wrapping. The words were in Kurdish. Our language, Shingali, is a dialect of Kurmanji, which is one of the Kurdish languages. Shingali is a mix of Kurdish and Aramaic words, a very old language of the Middle East. I recognized the candy labels, not just the lettering but also the shiny packaging. These were the candies Nafaa sold at his shop. Daesh hadn't just taken our money, cell phones, and jewels. They'd raided our stores.

Eivan grabbed two, tore off the wrapping, and popped them into his mouth. Adlan motioned for us all to sit. Another Daesh soldier was handing out headscarves, black and brown. He barked at us to put them on.

"Did you tell them anything?" my mother whispered to us when the soldiers had moved away.

"Like what?" Majida asked.

"I don't know. Something that would single you out? Make them remember you?"

I froze. The boy soldier would know who I was. He'd remember me talking back to him, asking questions.

"I told Daesh Eivan was my son," I said, my voice quivering. "The big man, directing things, from the classroom. I told him. I was afraid that the man was going to take Eivan so I picked him up."

"Good," Adlan cut in. "Good," she repeated. I relaxed a bit.

I couldn't take my eyes off my mother. It was as if I were seeing her for the first time. Dake had told me that Adlan was one of the most sought-after women in our tribe, the Mandki, when she reached marriage age. She hadn't been just physically beautiful with her long, brown hair and black eyes. She also had a quiet yet powerful presence. "Every man was in awe of her," Dake had said. "Men can be both afraid of and attracted to the power in women. And your mother allowed her power to move through her more than most. She was very close to the energy of Khatuna Fakhra."

"What will Daesh do if they find out about my lie?" I asked her.

"You can't let them know," Adlan replied sharply. "But don't worry," she added, her tone softening. "They won't ask. They can't see properly. You and Eivan are safer together." She looked around the garden to make sure there were no Daesh listening nearby. "I don't think we're going to Kurdistan," she said quietly.

"What about Hassan, Adil, Fallah?" Hadil asked, her voice trailing off. Adlan's spirits may have been rising, but Hadil's were sinking fast. Her shoulders were collapsed and she seemed smaller, almost like a child. She kept tying and untying a knot in the fabric of her dress.

Adlan shook her head. "I don't know what to tell you." We shimmied our bodies in closer. "I think," she started and then stopped. "I think we are . . . *you* are being sold." I could hear it in her voice: she was resigned to her own fate, but in whatever time she had left, she was going to give all she could to those around her, starting with us. Adlan was going to fight the darkness with light, sharing all the knowledge she had.

Eivan was lying on his back, happily playing a finger game, one that Adlan had taught my siblings and me when we were little.

"What are they selling us for?" I was trembling. I needed the answer, but part of me still didn't want to know.

Majida and my mother exchanged a look. Majida took over. "They'll sell the virgins . . . the girls . . . first," she said, shaking her head and wiping tears from her face. "Badeeah, what will happen to you is not love or marriage. It is abuse and violence and war . . . remember that."

Marriage. *Marriage.* I wanted to marry Nafaa. "Adlan," I interrupted, "I never told you, but I want to marry . . ." I was crying now, too.

"I know about you and Nafaa," my mother said. She stroked my face. "Hassan and I support your marriage to him when you're old enough. But for now, you will be walking down a dark tunnel. It's always darkest just below the light. You will be tested. Everyone in the world is tested in some way or another. This is your schooling now, Badeeah. You will emerge from this. That is a certainty. But what is not certain is when and how."

That's when I remembered Hassan's words from our trip to Shingal when I was five. "Your purpose in life is to hold onto love, so that darkness will eventually be succeeded by morning," my father had told me. I'd gotten my identification card, my Jinsiya, on that trip. I went to school that fall.

Daesh soldiers were now circling the garden, doling out rice and potato soup.

"Promise me," Adlan whispered, clutching my arm.

I nodded. "Anything. I promise you anything."

"Bring Eivan back safe."

Chapter Seven

Adrift

I awoke on a bus.

If you could call it being awake.

My eyes flickered open, then shut again. My head pulsed. It was a strain to remember anything. All I saw in my mind were images of men in black, the school at Kocho, the sandstorm that turned day into night, the guns . . . the man with the knife. I remembered promising Adlan I would keep Eivan safe.

Eivan was with me on the bus. But he, too, was waxing and waning, like the moon, awake and then asleep again.

I held him in my arms, rocking him like a baby,

pretending he was younger than he was so Daesh wouldn't take him away from me. From what I had seen in Kocho and Solakh, the youngest children were allowed to stay with their mothers. Older children they separated.

"My baby," I cooed whenever the men were near. "My baby boy."

My memory returned slowly, starting with Solakh. After the meal of rice and potato soup, Daesh had ordered us back inside the building, warning that bombers were coming. If they saw us, the airplanes would kill us all, claimed a Daesh man. There were maybe four hundred of us. Women, girls, and young children scrambled in from the garden, finding places along the cool corridors. Before sleep came rushing at me, I recalled asking Adlan, If the bombers were after Daesh, why would they bomb us? Were the Peshmerga, the Iraqi army, or the Americans coming to save us?

When I awoke next, I remembered Hadil and Majida being taken away. I had tried to sit up, but I was too weak to run after them. Adlan, however, found the strength. She rushed to her feet, screamed out their names, and scurried behind them.

They disappeared around a corner.

I heard gunshots, like I had back in Kocho. Rapid-fire, semiautomatic weapons.

Then silence.

Viyan, with her baby, had moved in close beside me, whispering that she thought Daesh was drugging our food. "They don't want us to fight back," she murmured.

"So that's why I am drifting," I said to her. "That's why I have no energy."

Then the long buses came.

Two or three of us were sharing each seat. We leaned into each other, floating in and out of each other's dreams and nightmares.

From time to time, I'd catch some of the Daesh men's words. "We're leaving fifteen women in Tal Afar. Forty from this bus to stay in Mosul."

The bus swayed like a boat as it slowed and stopped in the villages we passed. Men got on, walked around, and stared at us. If they pointed at a particular Yazidi girl or woman, she would be taken off the bus. One elderly man beamed with a toothless grin. "Who is going to marry me?"

One girl growled at him. "Who'd want to go with you, old man? You're older than our fathers!"

As I saw shame wash over his face, I realized a few men could still be reminded that what the Daesh men were doing was wrong. But they were too cowardly to protect us.

At the next stop, a boy wearing sports clothes hopped on the bus, jeering that we Yazidi were slaves now. "You're sabaya!" he crowed. The boy was even younger than the driver who had taken us from Kocho to Solakh.

The bus traveled by night. In the mornings, what I remember of them, we were led off the vehicle and corralled into schools in cities I had heard of but never visited. There, we were fed, usually plain white rice, sometimes noodles or biscuits. As the days wore on, the labels on the candies handed out to the children changed from Kurdish to Arabic. We drank water from the taps in the toilet rooms, which were overflowing with our waste, or from the buckets that Daesh left out for us. There were so many of us that often no spots were left on the floor to lie down. When that happened, we slept upright, our backs propping each other up.

At some point, I don't know when, Viyan and Ghalya and their babies were taken.

Eivan, when he was awake, didn't want me to sleep. He pleaded with me to keep my eyes open, maybe afraid that if I closed them, I wouldn't wake up. As my head drooped toward sleep, he'd prod and punch me, crying out for me to sit up and talk to him. "Tell me a story!" he'd demand. I was so exhausted, but I did what he asked, keeping the stories as short as I could. Sometimes I repeated the story of the founding of Lalish.

"After forty thousand years of sailing on wild seas, the angels came ashore, at Lalish . . ."

As Eivan and I moved across the desert, zigzagging like his football from one Iraqi town or city to another, I recognized the faces of girls and women I knew from

Kocho and other nearby villages—girls and women I had seen at weddings, funerals, and picnics and while on pilgrimage at Lalish. But we were never together for long.

When I was awake, my head and my burned leg seared like the hottest noon-hour sun during Chilé Haviné.

But even worse than the physical pain was the jolting, piercing knowledge that I was alone with Eivan. I didn't know whether my family were alive or dead.

On about day twenty-two, I began to see my mother— not in physical form, but I knew she was there. I felt her presence beside me. The first time she appeared, I recited in my head my promise that I would get Eivan safely back to Fallah and Samira.

After that, Adlan started to talk to me. Her voice was just a whisper at first. With a gentle nudge, she'd tell me, "Feed Eivan."

I began taking extra food for my nephew, and I'd give him some of mine, too. Adlan also told me things about the Yazidi. Maybe she'd told me those things when I was little, and I had forgotten. Or maybe she was really there. "Our people lived in Kocho for a thousand years," she said. "But we faced many genocides, so we moved to Shingal to be with other Yazidi. There is strength in numbers. In the 1970s, there were enough of us Mandki again to return to Kocho."

"Maybe your brothers were right," my mother told me another time. "Maybe we were too willing to accept our Arab neighbors. Maybe this is why we are suffering now. It is our punishment for not raising our voices. The Arabs under Saddam Hussein rewrote history, claiming they were the first inhabitants of the region. But the Yazidi, the Assyrians, the Christians, and the Jews lived in this area of Iraq long before Islam and the Arabs. The Arabs had their own land, Badeeah; they didn't need ours. It was Saddam's attempt to Arabize the country, so that he would be president for life, ruling over them and all the oil."

"Badeeah," I heard Adlan say on about day thirty. "Always move to the light. Don't let the darkness in. Remember the purpose of life. Hold onto love, so that darkness will eventually be banished."

❧

One afternoon I awoke on the bus, my head surprisingly clear.

I was sweating in the heat. The air stank from so many unbathed bodies nestled in tight together.

By the sun, I could tell it was about five and mid or late September. Eivan and I had been moving from town to town for at least a month. My body was awash with whatever drugs Daesh had been slipping in our food and water.

I looked down. Eivan's head was on my lap, his unwashed, oily hair sticking to his forehead. His breathing was raspy, as if he had a cold. I stroked his back and leaned my head against the window.

We were stopped on the road in front of a gas station, one large enough to fill up the oil tankers parked around it. In and among the cars and trucks, civilians in Muslim dishdashas, hijabs, khimars, and niqabs had set up roadside shacks where they hawked fresh fruits, juices, vegetables, secondhand electronics, and soaps. I was so thirsty, I could almost taste my favorite drink from the Shingal market: lemon ice water. There were so many Daesh mingling about. *If the Americans are going to bomb anywhere, this would be the place,* I thought to myself. *It's as if this is the Daesh barracks. Destroy their gas supply and destroy Daesh.*

I was sitting near the front of the bus. A Daesh guard a few seats ahead of me got on his cell phone, talking low and deep. "Yes. We're in Syria now," I heard him say.

My pulse quickened.

I looked out the window again, my eyes darting back and forth. The Daesh men walked with long strides and held their heads high.

They didn't feel threatened here. These men knew they had won the war. Whatever hopes I had had that the Peshmerga, the Americans, or even the Iraqi army were coming to rescue us vanished. Adlan had been right when she said I would be entering a dark tunnel. What I had never expected was that the darkness would be Syria, which was in the throes of its own civil war. How would I ever find the way home now?

∾

If I had had more energy, I would have encouraged the girls and women on the bus to rise up against our captors. As we moved into Syria, only the driver and one guard were with us on the bus. We weren't part of a convoy. Many times, our bus was the only vehicle on the road. The checkpoints we stopped at were manned by boys wearing Daesh-like clothing but carrying fake wooden guns. It hit me hard then that Daesh's numbers were not large. They were using children and model weapons to make their army look stronger and larger than it actually was.

As the bus moved into Raqqa, I couldn't help but notice that the colors were different than in Kocho, where just before Chilé Haviné, the region was green; then everything burned and turned to ash. Raqqa's buildings were white. They shone amidst sand that was bright yellow and gold. The sky was azure blue, like the seas I'd seen on nature programs. The roads were made of smooth black asphalt, not stones and dirt.

It was a Saturday, maybe, because the shops we passed were bustling. Women wearing niqabs and khimars hurried back and forth, weighed down by shopping baskets and bags. Children followed behind them, solemn-faced or skittish. The girls all wore headscarves, even the really young ones, and they stayed very close to their mothers. Men glanced at the bus and then quickly away.

In the only other large city I knew, Shingal, a gentleness wound its way around people. Even when it was busy, and even in the presence of soldiers, there was still order and calm.

Raqqa was nervous, as if it were surrounded by a wall people dared not step outside of, at least not for long. It was as if the city itself were trying to hide.

Chapter Eight

On the Other Side

Soft light warmed my face. I heard children laughing, followed by the chirping song of the nightingale.

I awoke thinking for a moment I was back in Kocho.

I sat up quickly, believing I was home.

Then my heart sank. I wasn't on a bus anymore, but I was far from Kocho.

I was in some sort of long building. For as far as I could see, there were bodies.

I was still a prisoner.

Some of the girls and women were awake. Most were asleep. As I looked at them, the floor felt as if it were falling out from underneath me.

My head began to spin.

I lay back down, steadying myself by scanning the metal beams that crisscrossed the ceiling.

From the way the light streamed in through a large window set high in the wall, I suspected it was midday. That baffled me. When Eivan and I were led off the bus into this building, it had still been light. I had heard the late afternoon Adhan, the Muslim call to prayer.

I estimated that I had been asleep for close to eighteen hours. Even when I was on the bus and drugged, the longest I had slept before waking was a few hours. Back in Kocho, I had been the first to sleep and the first to rise. I had an internal clock that saw me get exactly eight hours of sleep a night. I was up with the roosters. In the evening, if I had a test for school, I'd study until I drifted off, my head dipping down until it landed on the pages of the textbook I was reading. Adlan would poke my arm to wake me up. She'd hold my shoulders and guide me to the bedroom, where she had already laid out my mat and bedding.

Adlan. Sadness and longing rolled over me.

I curled myself into a tight ball, stuffed my fist inside my mouth, and, for the first time since my abduction, cried.

Hands stroked my back. Soft fingers wiped my hair from my face. I heard a female voice softly singing.

I relaxed a bit, thinking of Khatuna Fakhra.

Then I remembered Eivan. I pushed the hands away and lurched up. Despite still feeling lightheaded, I forced myself to stand, then walk.

Panic gripped me as I called out his name. I craned my neck across the sea of bodies.

"Eivan," I whisper-shouted.

Women looked up at me with defeated eyes.

Some began calling out Eivan's name, too.

Then I stopped cold in my tracks. Children were laughing at the very far end of the room. Tiny hands were clapping. I crept toward the sound, eventually seeing a group of small children playing patty-cake. Eivan was sitting in the middle of them, wearing a big smile.

"I thought you had disappeared," I said, falling down beside him. He looked at me, surprised.

Eivan and the other children were dirty. Their hair was tangled. They were all thin. But their eyes shone. It hit me that none of them knew what was happening.

I watched Eivan for a bit, then retreated to my original spot and pushed my back up against the wall.

"You're new here?" the woman beside me asked.

I looked over at her. She was lithe like Samira, Eivan's mother, and tall, too, judging from the way her long legs stretched out in front of her. She had an elegant neck, smooth skin, and high cheekbones set in a wide, welcoming face. But dark circles surrounded her eyes. Her hair was tied back but not with an elastic band. It was snarled with mud. Her irises were amber colored, speckled with white dots.

"Yes," I said. "I'm new here."

"I'm Navine," the girl said. "I'm from Tel Qasab."

I watched as Navine licked the palms of her hands and then ran them along the floor, picking up dust. She grabbed handfuls of cloth from her dress, burgundy with small yellow and white flowers, and squeezed. She then wiped her hands over her collarbones, neck, and cheeks, smearing herself in dirt.

"What are you doing?" I exclaimed, thinking she was crazy.

Navine let out a weak laugh. "The uglier you look," she said, "the less likely it is that the men will choose you."

"And the smell, too," I said, squeezing my nostrils together. Navine stank of body odor and bad breath.

Navine smiled, revealing dirty teeth.

"Sit like this when Daesh comes," she said, slumping. She dropped her head to one side and spread her legs open in front of her. She let her mouth hang slightly agape, then went cross-eyed.

I giggled weakly.

"They don't put as much of the sedative in the food here," Navine continued, sitting up straight again. "It's in the beginning, while you travel, that they drug you the most, so you're easier to transport. Like deadweight.

"There's a market they take the girls to," she continued. "They also sell us over the Internet. Men come here and look around, take who they want. Daesh thinks they're waging a war for Islam. They think they're shahids and freedom fighters," Navine scoffed. "They're capitalists. They're getting rich off kidnapping and selling us."

I stared at Navine, shocked at how calmly she could talk about what was happening to us.

"Aren't you afraid?" I finally asked, unsure what to make of this young woman.

"Of course," she said, leaning in close to me again. "But I try to push it away."

"My mother once said that fear is what ages us." A flood of sadness washed over me again.

Navine chuckled, then sighed. "I'm afraid all the time," she admitted. "But I know it won't help me. Whenever dark thoughts come to me, I try to remember something happy, like a brother's wedding or seeing my baby sister being born. I dream of the children I'll have one day, when I get out of here."

"What does Daesh do with the children?" I asked, my eyes floating to Eivan. "I mean, why have they taken the young ones?"

"I heard a rumor that Daesh got a young Yazidi girl to attach the wires on their bombs. She had small, nimble fingers. They kidnapped the mother, telling the child that if she didn't obey, *slit*." Navine imitated slashing her throat. I shrank back in shock.

I fell quiet. I wanted to protect Eivan. I wanted him to have a childhood. I wanted him to be far away from here.

"I've also heard that Daesh abducts children to kill for them," she continued, "to become suicide bombers. Child soldiers . . ."

"Is there any way to escape?" I asked her.

"I don't know of any yet, but I'll find one. In everything, there is a weakness, even these men. I'm being patient until I find out what it is. For now, I keep myself dirty, so when the buyers come, they don't want me."

I closed my eyes to rest them. Maybe I wasn't drugged anymore, but I was still very tired.

"I would like a son one day," Navine continued. I opened my eyes to see her gazing dreamily at Eivan. "When I get out of here, I will get married. I'm twenty-three, but when Daesh came around and asked my age, I told them I was thirty-one. They'll keep someone older like me to be a domestic slave. The really old women, they kill."

Eivan got to his feet and scanned the room, searching for me.

"I wanted to be a doctor," I said to Navine as I waved. Eivan jogged over and plunked himself down on my lap.

"Don't say *wanted*," Navine scolded, as a Daesh man in a dishdasha entered through a door not far from us, carrying a notebook. "Want!'"

I looked at her questioningly.

"You *will* be a doctor," she said. "Tell him that, too," she added, pointing to Eivan. "My advice to you: keep your dreams alive and separate from these men. The one thing they cannot take from you is your will to live. Only you can give that away."

∾

The Daesh man, a leader the soldiers addressed as Sheikh, shouted across the room that he wanted the new arrivals to identify ourselves. "I need your mothers' names and your ages and birthdays," he called out. "After that, we'll take your photographs."

I looked around nervously.

No one put her hand up.

Navine rolled her eyes. "When I first arrived, they said they wanted my mother's name to help reunite me with my sisters," she said in a low voice. "But I'm not so sure now. I think they want your mother's name so they can separate you from your siblings. Tell him you're older than you are. Tell him you're twenty-eight."

I gasped. "But surely they can tell I'm a teenager!"

"Just do it. Trust me. You look tired and bloated and much older than a teenager right now."

I kept my eyes glued to Navine as I slowly raised my arm. Sheikh moved through the bodies until he was in front of me.

My mouth grew dry as I debated whether I should lie and give him another name. "I am Badeeah," I finally told him. If there was a chance, even a glimmer of hope, that giving my real name would reunite me with my family, I wanted to be honest. He scribbled my name down in his book. "My father is Hassan."

"What is your mother's name?"

"Adlan," I said. My mouth was so dry, I couldn't swallow.

"How old are you?"

"Twenty-eight," I managed to get out. I felt faint being so close to this man. I was full of dread that he would discover my lies and take me away, like the men in Kocho took Manje.

"How many children do you have?" he asked.

"I am the daughter of Adlan," I repeated instead. I closed my eyes, hoping to stop my head from swaying. "I have one child," I finally said. "He's not quite two."

"This is him?" Sheikh said, pointing to Eivan, who was sitting still on my lap.

"Yes. His name is Eivan."

I averted my eyes quickly. Not only did I look like a teenager, Eivan most certainly looked older than two. He could form full sentences now, and his baby fat, except around the legs, was almost all gone.

Sheikh continued to write in his book. Finally, he grunted and turned, pausing momentarily before bellowing for the next woman to come forward.

Two girls stood up.

"You go over there," he said to me before moving toward them. He pointed at the door, where another Daesh soldier held a camera. I nodded.

As Sheikh moved away, I rolled onto my side and vomited.

Chapter Nine

In Between Heaven and Earth

After my photo was taken, I spent the afternoon staring at the ceiling.

On the way to Raqqa, the drugs Daesh had given us had at least dulled the pain.

Now, my rib cage was sore from vomiting. My right leg burned. My other leg ached from all the time I spent sleeping on buses or bare cement floors. Lifting my arms tired me. It hurt even to breathe. And that was just my physical body. My mind was tormented with doubts about whether I had done the right thing by taking Eivan. I went back in time, reimagining a different outcome in Hatimiya: Viyan, Ghalya, and I directing the driver to Kurdistan, where we would have been safe and the driver, a child-soldier, could have been rehabilitated.

Then I saw the faces of our Arab neighbors and of Abu Anwar. My family, my village, we had trusted those men. It made me feel even worse when I thought about Navine being from Tel Qasab, the very village where Khalil's truck had been pulled over. She was taken by Daesh on August 3, she said, likely just hours before we arrived there on the way back from the mountains. I couldn't help but think that Abu Anwar had let us return to Kocho, but had he stood by when she was taken and possibly even helped enslave Navine and the other Yazidi villagers?

I listened to Eivan playing with the other children until Navine called him back. She didn't want him leaving my side for long.

I half listened to Navine as she told Eivan folk stories to keep him occupied. I was grateful for her help with him, which gave me time to think. I finally had silence and a clear enough head to figure out what to do. But my thoughts careened into each other, leaving me with piercing migraine headaches. My eyes caught sight of a spider on an exposed ceiling beam. As I watched it, a deep heaviness grew inside me. That spider had more freedom than I did.

I heard Eivan tell Navine that he was building imaginary sandcastles, complete with moats, turrets, and drawbridges. I also overheard them playing a food game in which they each described their favorite meals. As they spoke, I imagined nibbling on Adlan's pastries.

When Eivan announced that he had to pee, Navine offered to take him, but I waved her away. I had promised Adlan I'd look after him. I wasn't honoring that pledge by feeling sorry for myself. Navine pointed to the back of the room and handed me a hijab.

"What's this for?" I asked. Daesh made us wear the hijab all the time. I was already wearing mine.

"You'll need it for another reason."

I cautiously placed one foot in front of the other, fighting through crippling fatigue and wooziness. Eivan's hand, locked inside mine, became slippery from my perspiration. I felt as if I had a fever. I wiped my fingers on my dress, reached down for Eivan's hand again, then stopped. I bent down instead and dragged my sweaty palms along the floor. When my palms were caked in dirt, I patted my face and then my dress, mimicking what Navine had done.

As we neared the urinal, I knew why Navine had advised me to bring the hijab: the smell. The toilet room, if you could call it that, had no door. The toilet itself, buried in the ground, had overflowed. Waste and urine spread out like a flooded riverbed. I coughed from the fumes and held one end of the hijab over my nose. Eivan put the other end up to his face. I was glad we still had our shoes on, though back in Kocho, we would never wear them inside. Leaving our shoes and boots at the door meant we were being conscious of cleanliness and keeping our prayer areas sacred. But Daesh didn't seem interested in etiquette.

By the time we made it back to Navine, the Isha, or the Muslim prayers for the night, had started. Many of the girls and women were now asleep.

My mind floated to Lalish as I heard Daesh in the other room murmuring their prayers. I imagined myself carrying the Chira, the sacred fire. At one point, Lalish had been constructed out of diamonds, gold, and lapis lazuli that corresponded with the energy that was present at certain times in the history of the planet. This is why Yazidi don't wear blue—it represents such a high spiritual color.

We now were living in the cycle of moon, which symbolizes immortality, enlightenment, and the exposure of the dark side of nature. It is believed that the energies are so strong in the moon cycle that wicked people who receive these energies will do very bad things. But those who are good receive this holy energy for good. It is a polarized time, the moon period. And indeed, the 20th and 21st centuries have been marred with wars, conflicts, and genocides of greater magnitude than ever before experienced on the planet.

In the moon period, the domes of our structures were made out of stone. The main building at Lalish had three structures, each representing a facet of the human experience: the body, the spirit, and the soul. "The soul is the center of life," Adlan had explained. "The spirit translates the language of the soul and gives it to the body." As I drifted in this dream state, I seemed to smell the dampness of the stones of the century-old building. I felt the energy of Khatuna Fakhra move through me, lifting me up. "Help me remain clear, so I can find a way to escape," I pleaded silently. "Watch over all the Yazidi who have been captured. No matter how far away I am, please keep me connected to Lalish."

Suddenly, I saw myself walking down a dark tunnel with a soft, flickering light at the end.

"Walk toward it," I heard Adlan say. "You and Eivan will live, my sweet daughter. Just keep walking toward the light."

∾

After morning prayers on day three, a young, fair-haired Daesh guard in a white dishdasha approached Eivan and got down on one knee.

I was angry. I wanted to fall back into my semiconscious position, staring at the ceiling, which was how I had spent the previous days. Instead, I went on high alert; anxiety about what this man was doing shot through me. I watched his long fingers—which I imagined in another time playing a beautiful instrument, like the *tambur*—

reaching into a box and pulling out chocolates. They were wrapped in crinkly yellow, green, and red cellophane, and I could see they had Arabic words on them. Eivan crept in close, and his eyes grew wide. The guard smiled as he passed him the sweets.

I moved to swat the candies away, but Navine stopped me.

The guard was helping Eivan unwrap one of the treats. As he did so, his hands trembled. I glanced at his face. The man's cheeks were flushed, and he seemed spooked about something.

When the guard got up to give chocolates to another child, Navine scolded me for looking directly at him. "Don't make him notice you any more than he already has," she snapped.

I snatched the chocolate from Eivan, who stared up at me in shock. I slapped a hand over his mouth to stop him from screaming. "I don't trust that man," I said to him sharply. "Don't touch it. It could be poison."

Navine pried my hand open, giving the chocolate back to Eivan. "Daesh doesn't drug the sweets," she said. "That's not what they're for. Let him enjoy something in these terrible times."

I ground my teeth as Navine wiped some chocolate from the wrapper over her face and her hair. She gestured for me to do the same.

"So far, whenever Daesh gives the children chocolate, the buyers come not long after," she explained. "The chocolate, I think, is to confuse the children so they think the men coming to look at their mothers are nice."

I spun Eivan around so his face was up against my chest. I told him to pretend to be sleeping. "In your head, work on your castle," I said.

"I'll make a sky castle now," he told me.

I molded my face into a smile.

The buyers came soon after, as Navine had predicted. "Do as I told you and they won't even notice you," she whispered. She spread her legs out in front of her and dipped her head to one side, staring out cross-eyed.

Some of the buyers wore dishdashas. Others sported Western-style jackets and slacks. Some were dressed in *kurtas* in rich purples, sky blues, and saffron over black pants. Some men's heads were adorned in turbans. As they moved along the floor, I picked up fragments of their Arabic, spoken in accents I didn't recognize, as well as languages I'd never heard before. Some of the men were old. Others were young, Fallah's age. Women, hoping like Navine and me to be unseen, shimmied their bodies away when the men approached them.

When an older man with a bald head and a gray beard pointed at two Yazidi girls about my age who looked related, a Daesh soldier yelled at them to stand. He ordered them to open their mouths, and the older man studied their teeth. The Daesh soldier next demanded the girls hold out their hands. The older man, dressed in a black dishdasha, examined their fingernails. Then he pulled up their dresses and looked at their legs. The girls were asked to turn around as the potential buyer gazed at their hair. I watched as urine dripped down one of the girl's legs, pooling on the floor.

The buyer nodded. As another Daesh soldier grabbed their arms, pushing them from the room, the girls locked hands. "This is not Islam what you're doing," one of them called out in rusty Arabic. "Please have mercy . . ."

The buyers and the Daesh soldiers snickered.

Another buyer picked a girl even younger than me, almost still a child. His voice carried through the room as he boasted to the others that he had found the perfect Yazidi *kafir*, which I knew was a derogatory word for a non-Muslim. "Allah has been kind to me, Inshallah," he called out. I cringed. I suddenly felt like I was going to be sick again.

It was hard to gauge how many were taken. Maybe twenty. Girls and women cried as they were led from the room. Some screamed. Navine moved in close, covered Eivan's ears with her hands, and mouthed to me that it wasn't over yet.

The wails came next from the floor above us. The terrifying, gut-wrenching calls of women and girls being raped.

I placed my hands on top of Navine's to further stifle the noise for Eivan. But I could feel that he heard as his body shook. The cries stopped when the Adhan announced midday prayers.

After prayers, the girls and women who had been taken away returned.

Their clothing was ripped, their hair was messy, and their faces were swollen with bruises and stained with tears. Some were limping.

I bled with them; parts of myself seeped out through my wounds. The only comforting thought I could muster was hope that the women and girls were hiding their dreams somewhere inside them. I wanted to tell them what Navine had told me: to safely tuck the best part of themselves somewhere far away.

Every few days, the buyers came.

The day after a girl or woman had been chosen and assaulted, she would disappear. Navine said they were sold to their buyers as slaves and then likely resold again and again.

"We are sabaya," Navine said, shaking her head. "In old times, when women and children were caught up in battle, the victor divided them among its soldiers to encourage them to keep fighting. It's as if the past two centuries don't exist for these men, as if they don't know that slavery has been abolished. We were not caught up in battle with our side being the loser. We were brutally kidnapped. These men are human traffickers. Most Muslims and mullahs say

Daesh is not Islam. If Daesh wins, the world will be a dark, horrible place."

I thought of my father then because he had said the same thing. My chest felt like it was caving in. I knew Hassan must be very worried about where all of us were. Fallah, too. Fallah must be worried sick about Eivan. I closed my eyes and prayed silently that a message had reached Fallah that Eivan and I were together.

"I pray, too," Navine said, startling me. My eyes popped open, and I looked at her questioningly.

"In my head, when I hear the Adhan," she continued. "I say our prayers, what I remember being taught of them. I didn't pray much until I was taken hostage. Now I pray all day long."

"I imagine I am at Lalish," I confided in her.

Eivan no longer played with the other children. Maybe the screams of the girls and women had scared him. He held onto me at all times. I could see by his panicked eyes that he was constantly afraid.

We ate the cold pasta, rice, and tomatoes we were served on plastic plates. But despite how much we ate, it was never enough. All three of us were fading. Our movements became slower and our speech more lethargic. I could feel my ribs, like sharp knives, starting to stick out.

∾

It was dawn. I'd been in Raqqa for about a month, I estimated, based on the evening Muslim calls to prayer that I had managed to count.

The rising light cast long, gray shadows on the walls. I wanted to wake Eivan, to tell him it was a good time for shadow puppets.

But then I stopped. I wasn't sure where I was. It was as if I was stuck in some hazy dream.

"You're in between life and death," I heard my mother say.

"Don't leave me," I whispered.

Adlan appeared in front of me then. She was wearing a white dress, just like the Faqras, the women who devote their life to spiritual enlightenment, did at Lalish. But a black sash was tied around her waist, indicating that someone had died. My mother looked young again.

"Are you dead?" I asked her.

She motioned for me to come.

I started to crawl toward her. Then I felt a hand grab my hair and pull me backward. It was the guard who had given candies to Eivan. Taking my arm, he yanked me to my feet and pushed me toward the other side of the room. Navine was stirring by now, with Eivan lying on the floor beside her. Seeing me, Eivan threw sleep off and kicked himself loose.

"Mama!" he was screeching as the Daesh guard led me from the room. "Mama!"

"I'll go back for the boy," I heard the guard say. "Just keep quiet for now." His hand, stinking of gasoline, covered my mouth.

Outside, the air was cool and infused with the aroma of baking bread. I heard dogs barking and women clanking pots as they started their morning fires, boiling water for tea and coffee. Men's shirts, children's pants, and a girl's dress shimmering with dew hung from a nearby clothesline.

The rising sun flooded over a barren field of swaying grasses. My eyes darted side to side, taking in my surroundings.

"I want to save you," the guard said into my ear. He removed his hand from my face. "I'm taking you somewhere where you and your son can be together."

Deep down inside me, a scream grew.

Chapter Ten

Awakening

Your mind plays tricks on you in captivity.

As the Daesh guard dragged me down the road, I remembered Navine's words from days earlier. I had been counting the cracks in the wall, thinking I might disappear into them, and she had slapped my cheeks until they stung. *Come back to the living! Come back!*

The guard quickened his pace as we rounded a corner, heading toward an old black car.

A pebble was stuck in my shoe. I asked the guard to stop so I could remove it. Once he did, I cemented my feet and then kicked him hard in the groin. His grip on my arm loosened. I slapped him across the face, then started to run, but he was too fast. He grabbed me from behind.

My eyes fell on a girl's dress on the clothesline. I remembered something I had heard back in the building. A woman had been talking to Navine about how, unlike Daesh in Iraq, who were mostly Iraqi Arabs supportive of Saddam Hussein, Daesh in Syria were foreigners. Most Syrian Muslims, the woman said, didn't support Daesh. Syrians wanted the fighting to end.

I screamed louder than I ever had before, hoping, praying, that someone, maybe the female owner of the laundry, would hear me and come to help.

The guard pushed me. I fell, stones digging into the palms of my hands, my knees, and the burn on my leg. I cringed from the pain shooting through me.

"We can make a home together," he said, leaning down close to my face. "Can't you see I am trying to help you?"

"No," I yelled. "Not without my son."

"You have my word I will go back and get him. Just do not make any noise."

I stared at him, panting. "How can I trust you? You people have lied to us from the beginning."

The guard reached down to give me a hand, then suddenly stepped off to one side. Behind him emerged two Daesh soldiers.

I stayed on the ground, averting my eyes.

The guard, speaking fast, explained that he had been

ordered to take me somewhere. "Ask Emir," he said, using the Arabic word for ruler or commander.

"Don't lie! You're taking her for yourself," one of the soldiers charged.

I heard a whizzing sound, a fist moving through the air, then a thump.

I glanced over and saw the guard lying on the ground. He was holding his stomach where the soldiers were kicking and punching him.

Hands grabbed me under my armpits, pulling me up. One of the soldiers continued to beat the guard while the other shoved me in the direction we had just come from.

As we walked, I strained to look around. The cement building where we were being held was tall and long, maybe an old factory or farm. I could see at least three stories. Its large windows were covered in metal bars or boarded up. There was nothing much around us except fields and a few homes.

Back inside the building, the soldier forced me down a short corridor, then into a room where Daesh soldiers were drinking tea, eating, and smoking. About half a dozen men lounged on chairs and sofas. A large-screen television was tuned to an Arabic news channel.

The smell of their food made me nauseous. I pulled my hijab tight around my face, curving my shoulders inward.

I heard a door creak open.

"This is Emir," said the soldier, pushing me from behind.

My knees buckled. I dug my nails hard into my palms, hoping the pain would stop me from fainting.

The man called Emir stepped in front of me. I kept my eyes down, noticing that the cuffs of his green army pants were speckled with mud.

Emir ordered me to hold out my trembling hands.

As he examined my fingernails, I felt bile moving into my throat. I forced it back down.

Emir spun me around, slipped off my hijab, and looked at my hair.

"You're dirty," he exclaimed, clacking his teeth.

I said nothing. I kept my eyes steady on the ground. My body was shaking. I was sure I was going to urinate on myself the way I had seen other girls do.

"One of the guards wanted her for himself," the soldier behind me said.

"How old are you?" Emir snapped.

"Twenty-eight," I mumbled. I was so frightened now that my teeth were chattering.

"You look younger," Emir said. "I know these Yazidi sabaya are lying about their ages. I want the buyers to see her when they next come."

He then motioned for me to be returned to the others.

∾

As soon as the door to the big room swung shut, Eivan ran up to me, his face swollen and drenched in tears. He flung his arms around my legs.

I bent down and picked him up, hobbled back to Navine, and collapsed beside her. Eivan opened his tiny hand to show me five chocolates, mashed and melted. "The guard left them for me. He said he was going to take you out first and then we'd be a family."

I bit back a cry of anguish. What had I done? Maybe the guard had been our freedom after all, and I had blown it. I closed my eyes and breathed slowly.

"I want us all to escape," I told him. "We can't leave without Navine. Next time, she goes with us."

Eivan, exhausted from all his crying, soon fell asleep.

After I recounted what had happened, I told Navine the time for us to escape had come. "Outside, there are fields, as far as I could see. The guard led me out a back door, not through the front where the Daesh soldiers stay. I saw laundry, a girl's dress. Surely a mother would help us if she knew we were being held against our will."

Navine leaned back against the wall and closed her eyes.

I shifted in close to her. "I may have found the weakness in these men. The guard"—I pressed on—"when the guard comes back, I'll tell him I want to leave with him." My heart was beating fast. We had to escape before the next round of buyers came. "I'll tell the guard I will go with him willingly, but that he has to take all of us. I'll tell the guard you're my sister."

Navine's eyes popped open. "You'd do that for me?"

"Yes. You looked after Eivan when I couldn't. You tell me things I need to know."

"The guard may do things to you, Badeeah," Navine said, shaking her head.

"He seems different. He's not respected by the others. If I can get him to take us out of the building, maybe he'll let us go. Maybe he'll even help us return to Iraq. It's our only hope."

Navine's lips were quivering. "If you're sold and Eivan is left behind, I'll say he's my son. I'll watch over him if you can't. I will get him home to his mother. But if you and Eivan can escape, go . . . leave me behind. Don't wait for me. Don't make the guard take me too."

I blinked back tears. Navine had become more than a sister. In that moment, I didn't know where I began and she ended. We had become one. Wherever I went, she would be with me, about that much I was certain.

Five new women arrived later that day.

My heart pounded. One of them, I was sure, was a relative of ours named Salwa. I waved. Salwa looked right past me. It was as if she didn't see anything at all.

I inched toward her. There was something about her appearance that gave me chills. But there was no doubt in my mind about who she was.

"Salwa?" I said when I drew in close. My voice was wobbly.

When Salwa turned toward me, I could see that her dark-brown pupils were enlarged. She was still drugged. One of her eyes was swollen and red.

I gathered up my skirt and sat down beside her.

Salwa parted her dry, cracked lips. But no words came out. She looked into my eyes intently.

"Where have you been?" I asked. She flinched as I touched her bruised cheek.

Her lips trembled and parted again. "We were sold at market, like goats. Because I had never been with a man, I was sold for the highest price. But I don't want to talk about that," she said in a distant voice. "How did you end up here with Eivan?"

So she'd recognized us after all. "Daesh thinks he's my son."

Salwa grabbed my hand, squeezing my fingers. "They've killed the children. I've seen it. I've seen them do it. I miss home so much . . ."

I stared at Salwa's battered face, waiting for her to continue. After a long silence, her eyelids fluttered.

"When were you taken?" she asked.

"August 15 . . ." Just remembering the date caused my skin to burn. "Daesh first came the day after Chilé Haviné. They knew we would all be home celebrating."

"I was caught on August 8, trying to escape to the Shingal Mountains," she told me.

"I don't know where Adlan or Hassan are, or Fallah . . ."

"I don't know where anyone is either, Badeeah."

"Salwa," I said, touching her shoulder gently, "you need to remain strong. I know they are doing terrible things to you, but you need to keep your hopes and dreams safe, hidden, inside you. Most of all, keep them alive."

"I want to leave," she whispered. "I want . . ." Her eyes welled.

"We all want to go home," I said softly. "And we will."

"No," she murmured, shaking her head. "You don't understand. I want to die."

The hinges on the main door squawked. Daesh was coming. I looked over, hoping it would be the guard. But it was the man the soldiers called Sheikh.

"You can't give up, Salwa." I wanted to tell her of my visions of Adlan. I wanted to convince her to stay alive.

"You need to remember a number," Salwa said as Sheikh stopped in front of one of the new girls. "Please, Badeeah. Listen carefully. The number is 07500851411. Repeat it back to me now."

"07500851411," I said slowly, rolling the digits off my tongue. "But what is this number?"

"Ameen's. It is Ameen's cell phone." Ameen was a distant cousin of ours. "He's with other Yazidi who are coming to get us. Find a phone, call him."

Once I understood how important the number was, I decided to use a trick I knew to commit it to memory. I associated each digit with a birthday or a special holiday. The first four digits of the phone number were the same for most of Iraq. I could remember to add another zero, and after that, the eight followed by a five stood for my birthday: the eighth of May. I was fourteen when I realized I had feelings for Nafaa. Both Eivan's birthday and my parents' wedding anniversary were in November, the eleventh month.

"Now go," Salwa said, shoving me away. "Don't let Daesh see you close to me. These men don't like relatives being together."

Within an hour, Daesh had come and taken Salwa. She departed the way she had come: like a ghost.

Chapter Eleven

Immortal

Whenever I heard the room's main door open, my pulse quickened. Part of me was hoping it would be the guard; another part of me was terrified that it would be him and I'd have to go through with my plan.

But neither the guard nor the buyers came. As the days wore on, I grew nervous. What if Daesh had ordered the guard never to come back? What if they had killed him for trying to take me? What if I had missed our one chance at freedom?

I realized one day that in my daydreams about my homecoming with Eivan, I had forgotten what the people close to me looked like, even Adlan. Unless her spirit was standing in front of me, I found it hard to picture her face, the lines of her neck, the curves of her body.

I confided this to Navine one night. "Majida, Fallah, Hadil, Adil, Hassan . . . even Dake," I said to her. "I can't see their faces anymore. What if I don't recognize them? What if they were never real?"

Eivan was still awake, lying on his stomach beside Navine and me. On impulse, I handed him his toy taxi. It was the first time I had dared to bring it out. But Daesh had only one guard on duty, and he was sitting at the far end of the room, near the toilet, because a girl had tried to hang herself there the day before with her hijab. The guard's legs were spread apart, and his head was lolling back and forth. He let out an occasional snore. I lectured Eivan about not making any noise and cautioned him only to move the taxi a few inches along and then back again.

Clearly, my nephew had also been listening in on our conversation.

"Babo has whiskers," Eivan said, referring to Hassan. "When he puts me on his lap, he flutters his eyelashes against my cheek. He calls it butterfly kisses."

I smiled, remembering how Hassan had done that with me, too, when I was little. Recalling it gave me an idea.

"Let's play the finger game," I said to Eivan.

He parked the taxi next to my leg, then perched himself in front of me, locking his fingers together.

Navine was starting to drift off. "How do you play?" she asked groggily.

"I point to a finger and Eivan tells me who lives in that house," I explained. "But let's add a twist. Let's say something we remember about the people who live in the house."

The first house was Eivan's home in Shingal.

"Baba has warm hands that cuddle me and peppermint breath," Eivan began.

I laughed, remembering how much Fallah liked mint candies. Then it was my turn. "Fallah is aware of everything going on around him. Just like you," I added, ruffling Eivan's hair. "He never makes enemies. He's liked by everyone."

"Mama next," Eivan said excitedly. "Mama makes me safe. She smells like flour, too."

"Samira has a kind heart," I said about his mother. "She is soft-spoken and patient."

"Mama is soft like the coat of a deer," Eivan added.

As we went on playing, I realized it no longer mattered that I had forgotten people's faces. Who they were, their essence, was much more important.

"Majida," I said to Eivan, "is bold. She is modern. She is forward thinking, encouraging girls to have their own identities. Hadil is a billowy, fast-moving cloud on a sunny day. Adil shows people the way. Adlan is like warm bread, pomegranate molasses, an angel."

Another night, Navine and I stayed awake talking, keeping one another's spirits up by imagining the future. She was curious about why I wanted to be a doctor, so I explained it to her.

"You remember the 2007 bombings?"

Of course, she did. Everyone remembered those bombings. Extremists had driven fuel tankers and cars packed with explosives into the center of two Yazidi towns not far from Kocho, killing hundreds. The attack had started when Muslim gunmen, possibly the Islamic State, stopped a bus in Mosul. They ordered the Christians and Muslims off, then killed the remaining twenty-three Yazidi passengers.

"Some of the wounded from the bombings," I said, "streamed into Kocho, seeking the help of our one overworked doctor, Elias Salih. Like I often did as a child, I was sitting on the side of the road, keeping an eye on his office. Sometimes I read a book while I sat there, but this time I just watched the injured men, women, and children waiting outside, their blood dripping on the dusty road. People were quiet, cradling their broken arms, as if they accepted that they might die before the doctor could see them. I finally couldn't take any more. I ran home and brought back sheets and towels, buckets and soap. I helped clean dirt off people's wounds while the patients with more serious injuries went in first. My father later told me that many people died who could have lived if only

Kocho and the other Yazidi villages had more doctors. That was the day I knew I wanted to care for others."

"You'll be a doctor," Navine said in a quiet voice. "Just like I will be a mother to a son one day."

Chapter Twelve

The Dark Room

Then one day, the guard who had taken me outside the compound was back.

Everything inside me told me to look away, to run away, to abandon my plan. But when the guard knelt to give Eivan chocolates, I shuffled up close beside him. "I'll go with you," I croaked.

His body stiffened.

"I want to go with you," I repeated. "Get me out, and my son and my sister, and I will do whatever you ask. But you need to take us all."

The guard scanned the room, then let the contents of the candy box fall. Chocolates and sweets scattered everywhere. I realized he had dropped them on purpose to give us a cover for talking.

"I didn't know if I could trust you," I told him. "Now I do. I want to be with you. But we don't have a lot of time. Emir says he wants the buyers to see me when they next come."

"I understand," he said.

When the guard moved on to the next child, I tore open the wrappers on Eivan's chocolates. Navine and I rubbed the wrappers all over us. We even smeared chocolate on our teeth to make them look stained.

Neither of us heard the footsteps approach.

From out of nowhere, someone yanked my hair. I screamed as I felt myself being hauled up off the ground and then dragged along the floor.

Pain pulsated across my head and down my neck. Even my teeth hurt, as if they were being ripped from my body. I twisted from side to side, trying to break free, but the attacker's grip was too strong.

I heard Eivan chasing after me. "Hide!" I tried to shout to him. But my throat was too sore for words to come out.

In a second-floor room, I was beaten and called names.

Afterward, I curled myself up in a ball on the dirty floor.

"In a few days you will leave," Emir shouted down at me. He twisted my arm behind my back until the pain was so searing that I couldn't see. The words "Yazidi whore" were the last things I heard before I passed out.

When my eyes flickered open again, there was nothing but darkness around me. I was lying on my back and I could hear myself breathing.

My scalp tingled. As I tried to sit up, pain ricocheted through me. My legs and chest were on fire.

I felt my lips. Swollen. I patted my face. My cheeks and eyes were puffy, too.

I lay back down, staring up at the darkness.

Then I sensed a body beside me. I heard a moan. It was Navine.

"Are you all right?" I called to her quietly. My mouth felt stiff, and I could taste blood.

"Yes," she said. I could hear her coughing. "They beat us both."

"Eivan," I said. "Where?"

"I don't know."

Despite the pain that throbbed in every part of my body, I pulled myself to my feet, bracing myself against the concrete wall. I felt my way to a metal door and pulled on the knob, but the door was locked.

I banged my fists against the metal, screaming for someone to come.

"Where is my son?" I yelled.

No answer.

No footsteps or voices.

"Where are we?" I called to Navine. "Did you see where they were taking us?"

"No."

It was somewhere dank. The air was full of moisture as if we were underground. Walking stiffly, I felt my way around the room: buckets, brooms, sponges, and a mop. I found a towel and knelt to place it under Navine's head.

"They said they had been watching us. They knew we were making ourselves ugly," Navine said. "I should have warned you."

"About what?"

"The guard. He might have wanted you for himself, but he was angry after the soldiers beat him. He felt you had betrayed him. I should have known that he would never trust you again. But I guess I wanted to believe in him, too."

For the first time since I had met Navine, I heard her crying. Softly, I sang her a lullaby Adlan had sung to me as a child.

When I could hear that she was asleep, I lay back and listened to the silence.

No words. No sounds coming from the other side of the door.

No water to drink. No cold pasta. No rice. No chocolates. No buyers.

No Eivan.

I slept, then paced. I wasn't sure for how long. Hours? Days?

I banged on the door.

I tugged at the knob from time to time, hoping it would eventually yield.

I screamed for Eivan. I begged Adlan to appear and tell me what to do. But she never came nor did I hear her voice.

The silence was deafening.

∾

I shielded my eyes with my hands as light flooded into the tiny room.

"Get up. You're leaving," a man ordered. I recognized the guard's voice.

"Where is Eivan?" I demanded.

No response.

"Where is my son?" I repeated, pulling myself up from the damp floor.

Still nothing.

The guard threw khimars and niqabs at Navine and me and told us to put them on.

The guard was angry, like Navine had said. I had wounded his ego. Now he'd rather see me dead than consider helping us.

When we stepped outside, I could see that we had been locked in a basement, probably a cellar for storing crops.

Outside, the air was drier, cool, and biting. I wrapped my sweater around me. Autumn had come. In a few weeks, in my old life, my Kocho life, my family would have been going on pilgrimage to Lalish. I imagined roasting apples and pears from the orchards.

Finally, I could hear sounds again: men talking, birds, dogs barking.

I racked my brain for something I could say to get the guard back on my side.

But then I heard a small voice call out, "Mama." I turned in one direction and then the other. The niqab covered my entire face except for my eyes. I had never put one on before, so, as I fumbled to adjust it on my face, I couldn't see.

"Mama!" the voice called again.

A hand slipped under my armpit, and I felt myself being hoisted up through the open door of a small bus or minivan. I smelled stale cigarette smoke as the same hand guided me to sit on the floor.

Then I felt a tiny, warm hand slip into mine.

I pulled the niqab away from my eyes to see Eivan beside me. A bruise pulsed purple and red on his cheek.

I pulled him in close as tears welled up, tears I didn't even know I'd stored away. Tears of love.

Chapter Thirteen

The American

"Where are we going?" I asked as the minivan lurched forward.

"Aleppo," said the Daesh man in the passenger seat.

There were ten Yazidi in the vehicle, six women and four small children, including Navine, Eivan, and me, as well as a Daesh driver and a guard.

It was dusk, maybe 5:00 p.m. Our driver, from what I could make out, was another teenager. He had a sparse beard, like the fur of a baby goat, and pimpled cheeks. *A boy*, I thought, *who if he lived in another place might have been at school or at football practice.*

The Daesh guard had light eyes, maybe blue or green, though it was hard to tell in the light. His eyelids drooped at the corners.

There were no seats in back. The ten of us sat on the metal floor of the minivan surrounded by empty cigarette packages, crumpled papers, and candy bar wrappers.

The vehicle was from the 1970s and had been shipped to Syria from Europe for its final years of life. "We're a giant charity shop, us and other war zones in the world," Adil had said one day after the Americans came to Iraq. "The world dumps its garbage here and calls it 'aid.' What we need is peace, not their old running shoes." In Kocho, it had been a big deal for my father to be able to drive an old BMW. It meant he was important. In North America, his vehicle would have been discarded as junk.

"What will happen to us in Aleppo?" I asked the guard.

He kept chewing his gum, ignoring me.

About fifteen minutes into the drive, the minivan pulled into a long tunnel and stopped.

The men in the van rolled the windows down. A large Daesh man, wielding a knife like the ones the elders used to slaughter our goats at festivals, materialized from the tunnel and moved in close.

"Yazidi sabaya?" he snarled. His accent was unfamiliar, maybe North African.

The Daesh guard in the front seat grunted.

"Good! I'll behead them all right now!"

"What did they say?" Navine whispered. The other women looked at me in terror. I swallowed the lump in my throat. None of them understood Arabic.

"I don't know," I stammered, unable to tell them that we were about to die.

The guard in front began to argue with the knife carrier, telling him we were meant for someone named The Commander. We had been sold to an emir. The large man took a few steps back, waving his knife around. I could tell by the way it swooshed that it was sharp.

Finally, another Daesh man in a white dishdasha arrived. He cocked his hand pistol and waved it at the man with the knife, shouting at him that the sabaya were not to be touched.

Within minutes, our minivan was moving forward. Once the van was safely through the tunnel, it sped up quickly, as if we were running away.

About an hour into the drive, we reached a checkpoint. I managed to read one of the signs I saw through the window: Dayr Hafir. Cars, trucks, minibuses, and large transport buses lined both sides of the road like fences. We watched as Daesh soldiers swarmed some of the vehicles, ripping open suitcases, boxes, and bags. Clothing flew up in the wind, caught in the daze of the headlights, then somersaulted along the road like tumbleweeds. Syrian families stood off to the side, watching, stone-faced and shivering. They were refugees, fleeing a country diseased by civil war. Aleppo was spitting out its own people. The city was a battlefield.

Long before we reached Aleppo, we could see the pollution hugging the city. Smoke from burning buildings and particles from explosions sifted their way into the vents in the van, making us cough. Our driver had to skirt the debris littering the roads. For many miles, we moved at a crawl.

Finally, our minivan entered a residential area. Some of the houses were mansions with gated fences, gardens, and fountains. Most of all, I noticed the trees.

My thoughts drifted to the oak, linden, elm, and ash trees that grew densely around the Shingal Mountains and Lalish. Hassan would hunt for the Zagros oak tree with the widest branches, for shelter from the rains, and my brothers would set up our food and tents there. Afterwards, Hassan rolled his cigarettes, humming folk songs. Adlan would make flatbread over a bonfire. When Dake was still alive, she would sit with her legs curled underneath her, sucking on pomegranate seeds, telling Khudher and me stories. "This part of the world, Mesopotamia, is the cradle of civilization," she would say. "But that isn't just because this is where civilization began. It is also because, in the silence of nature, the spiritual could become part of the world. Every river leads to the sea, and the sea leads to every river."

∽

The minivan pulled up in front of a mansion flanked by tall, white pillars.

The Daesh guard in the passenger seat snapped at us to straighten our headscarves.

When we got out, the street was empty. The air was thick, like it had been in Raqqa. I could see lots of alleyways along the street. Many people's windows were open despite the cooler air. I caught sight of a black-veiled woman on a second-floor balcony.

I picked up Eivan, who wrapped his legs around my torso.

A wrought-iron fence surrounded the house, an open padlock dangling from one of the bars. We entered a courtyard full of dead, crackling bushes.

Inside, the house smelled of camphor, cinnamon, mint, and cardamom, as if someone had just finished cooking. The Daesh guard instructed us to keep our headscarves on. Once we had taken off our shoes, he led us down a hallway lit dimly by a fluorescent light bulb. Navine wrung her hands together, and Eivan tightened his hold on me. The other women crept in close, asking me in Shingali what was going on. I had no answers for them.

The dusty furniture was made of heavy wood. The place had not been cleaned in a long time. The carpets were scuffed. On the walls hung framed posters featuring quotes from the Quran.

A new man with a slight build appeared, taking over for the guard from Raqqa.

"I'm al-Amriki's translator," the man said, leading us into the kitchen. I translated for the others, stumbling briefly over the words *al-Amriki*.

I knew these words.

They meant "the American."

I cleared my throat. "Are you the man who bought us?" I asked.

"No."

"Is the man we've been sold to American?"

"Yes," the new man said. "He is the Sheikh of Aleppo."

I stood in stunned silence.

Americans were supposed to free us. If America was part of Daesh, how would we ever be rescued?

"Tell the others," the translator said, "that they need to wash. Sheikh wants everyone clean, even the children."

As al-Amriki's translator led the other women and children to the shower room, Navine found a pot and began to boil water for tea. I watched the flame on the gas stove rise. Beside the stove was a sink with running water. Pots and pans dangled from a circular hanger attached to the ceiling.

In a half-opened drawer, I spied spoons but no knives. I put Eivan down on the floor just as al-Amriki's translator returned carrying a small cutting knife. He pointed to a brown bag of rice and some overripe tomatoes and eggplants sitting on the table. "I will watch while you cut the vegetables," he said to me. "Sheikh is an important man. You need to wear headscarves in the house because there are many meetings here. You women will make food for the men. But you will not serve it. The food gets left at the door of the guest room."

"Is this important man really from America?" I asked.

"Yes," said the translator. "He saw that in America, people have lost their way. He came to us knowing we were the answer. He is an emir, one of the greatest and most beloved. *Hamdulilah.*" Praise be to God.

My head was swimming with questions I knew better than to ask. Instead, I listened as the translator outlined the house rules.

We were to do all the cooking and cleaning. Eivan was supposed to help, too. If we needed supplies, we were to tell the translator or one of the guards, and they would get them at the market. We were supposed to bathe every day. Before prayers we were to wash our hands and feet. At all times in the house, Navine and I had to wear the hijab. The translator passed me a Quran. "You're to pray when you hear the Adhan. You must stop what you are doing and pray."

I stared at the book wide-eyed. It was bound in black leather that was cracked in places.

"What is it? Didn't they show you in Raqqa how to be a Muslim?"

I shook my head.

"Ahhh, they were keeping you to be a slave. A Muslim can't have another Muslim as a slave," the translator explained. "In this house, you will be free. Repeat after me. 'There is no God but Allah. Muhammad is His messenger.'"

I stared at the man.

"Say it," he barked. Slowly, I repeated it, knowing full well I was repeating Islamic words. I was saying the Shahada, what people say when they convert to Islam.

"Good," he said when I was done. "You are a Muslim now."

"I don't want to be a Muslim," I started to say. But before I could get the words out, the kitchen door flew open so fast and hard it banged against the wall.

The man who entered the kitchen spoke choppy Arabic, informing the translator that the women were not yet bathing.

"Go tell them to wash or they will not be fed," the translator ordered me. I had taken a few steps toward the door when the new man put his hand up for me to stop.

"I am al-Amriki," he said.

I kept my eyes on the floor. He spoke Arabic from the front of his mouth, not his throat like a native speaker.

The man tilted my face up toward him until our eyes locked.

"What is your name?" al-Amriki asked.

"Badeeah," I mumbled.

He let go of my face, and I looked down again. "You will soon discover that everything you believe about your religion is wrong. That angel of yours, he is Iblis, the devil. You have been misled."

"Who is this?" al-Amriki asked, tapping the top of Eivan's head. I flinched. I didn't want him to touch Eivan.

"My son," I whispered.

"I have decided to take you as my wife."

He moved in so close to me I could feel the heat rising from his body.

"We're slaves," I stammered. "Not wives."

"She's a Muslim now, like you asked, and young," al-Amriki's translator cut in. "Maybe sixteen, although, like the others, she lied. She told them in Raqqa she was twenty-eight." Al-Amriki and the translator laughed.

I began to perspire.

"I am twenty-eight," I said in a low voice.

"I will sell you to my friend," al-Amriki continued. I glanced up to see him pointing at Navine. "And the pregnant woman, I'll sell her to an old man. Once the baby is born, he can take her as his wife."

A car door slammed outside. I heard gunshots far away, then the distant whirring of a helicopter.

"I'm married," I said quickly. "You can't marry me. I'm married to another man."

The room fell silent. This time I could hear water running in the shower room down the hall and women speaking to each other in Shingali.

"It's *haram*," I said hesitantly, struggling to remember what I knew about Islam. From school and from overhearing Hassan's friends, I knew *haram* meant forbidden. It was haram for the Muslim men visiting my father to drink alcohol, which Yazidi do at parties. I also knew it was haram to marry a girl married to another man.

He scowled and then leaned in close. "I'm not stupid like the Mujahdeen in Iraq and Raqqa," he said in a low voice so no one else could hear. "I can tell your age, and I can tell you're a virgin. That child isn't even your son."

My head started to spin. To steady myself, I silently recited the number that Salwa had given me in Raqqa, 07500851411.

"Come with me," al-Amriki said, grabbing Eivan and heaving him over his shoulder. "You come with me, too," he ordered, grabbing my wrist.

The shower room had a bathtub and a sink with a mirror. One wall was covered in beige ceramic tiles. Even though there was mold in the cracks, the tiles twinkled under the light of an ornate ceiling fixture. I could hear dripping from the leaky showerhead.

Al-Amriki yanked my niqab off and ordered me to look at him.

He had wavy, black hair and muddy brown eyes. Thick lips and high cheekbones. His beard ran down the sides of his face and met under his chin. His skin was blotchy white, not brown, as if it had never seen the sun before.

Hassan, when he was canvassing to become a politician, had said that a great leader was not one who dictated and used force but someone who made others believe in themselves. Al-Amriki struck me as someone who made everyone around him afraid.

Chapter Fourteen

A Cave in the Clouds

I was wedged on the kitchen floor with Navine on one side and Eivan on the other. The other women were preparing food and tea for al-Amriki and two male guests, who even at this late hour were no doubt talking about war.

I felt the weight of the entire city of Aleppo on top of me.

Al-Amriki had said he would come for me once his meeting was over. I had a sudden urge to tell Navine about my life, as if I might not be coming back.

"I started school when I was five," I began. "I followed my sisters Hadil and Majida to the schoolhouse. They wouldn't let me walk with them at first, saying I would be sent away as soon as the teacher found out my age." My mind drifted back to Kocho, and my eyes swelled. Navine reached over to take my hand.

"The headmaster, who was a friend of my father's, studied me and then my identity papers. Finally, he let out a laugh. 'You can stay and watch,' he told me. 'But you can't pass any subjects. Not until next year.'"

Eivan had pushed his body in close to mine, listening intently.

"I loved learning to read and write," I said. "At home, at night, I would study and study. Somehow, I managed to convince my teacher to let me write the first test. I got a perfect score, so he allowed me to write another and then another. Most of all, I liked learning Arabic. At home, I would watch Arabic programs on the television to help me study."

Navine squeezed my hand tightly. "I may need to leave the room for a while," I murmured to Eivan. "But Navine will look after you. When I was little like you, my toys were made from dirt. Until Adlan made me a doll, I'd mold dolls from mud using leaves for hair, nuts for eyes, flower petals for shaping into mouths. Promise me you will use your imagination and never stop playing. Whenever you need to, you can go somewhere in your mind and you will be safe."

"Tell me a story?" Eivan pleaded. "Please . . . story."

"Well, let's see. Mir Meh was a man who tried to run away from death," I began. "When he was very young, he left his family in a village much like Kocho to live with a woman named Falak."

"Mir Meh means prince," Eivan whispered.

"That's right. Falak was a witch, and she promised to make Mir Meh immortal, which means he would live forever. Falak and Mir Meh spent a long time living in a cave high up in the Shingal Mountains, close to the clouds, where no one could see them. They were very happy, so happy that Mir Meh didn't realize how much time had passed. One day, feeling heaviness in his heart, he told Falak he wanted to visit his family. He missed them."

Tears trickled down my cheeks as I thought of Adlan, wishing she were here to guide me. Eivan didn't belong here, none of us did, in this place of guns and bombs and men who stank of hatred. I thought of gurgling streams, soft grasses, ferns, mosses, and the butterfly that had led me to safety when I was small.

"Falak let Mir Meh know that it had been five hundred years since he'd left his family, and that even if he went in search of them, he wouldn't find anyone still alive. Mir Meh wanted to go anyway, so Falak gave him three apples and a horse. 'Keep these apples,' she told him. 'Eat them or save them, but don't give them away.' Mir Meh promised Falak he would do as she said.

"Mir Meh arrived at his old village, but there was no one he recognized, just like Falak had warned. A man who introduced himself as Bako greeted him. Bako washed down Mir Meh's horse and listened to Mir Meh's story about living in the mountains with a witch who had made him immortal. When Mir Meh mentioned the apples, Bako secretly wondered if they would make him immortal, too. He begged to be given one of the apples to cure his sick brother. Mir Meh, having forgotten Falak's words and his promise to her, agreed. Within seconds of Bako taking his leave with the apple, Mir Meh and his white stallion weakened.

"Not long after, Bako returned. This time he approached Mir Meh disguised as an old beggar woman and convinced Mir Meh to give him the second apple. As Bako took his leave, Mir Meh and his horse became frail.

"Bako returned a third time, this time disguised as a beautiful young woman. She told Mir Meh her mother was dying from a terrible disease. Mir Meh, still failing to remember Falak's words, gave his last apple to Bako.

"Shortly after that, Mir Meh and his horse died. And Bako, who had eaten all three apples, became immortal."

Eivan stayed quiet.

I could hear gunshots in the distance again. *If only we could magically pass through the wall, we'd be free,* I thought. Someone was fighting these men. If we could find them, we could go home.

I continued talking over the lump in my throat. "Mir Meh was my favorite story when I was your age. Your aunts and I would roll our mats out on the floor and lie close together to keep warm as we listened. Each time Adlan told the story, we would help her come up with a different ending. One version was that when Mir Meh descended from the top of the mountain, he passed through a dark cloud that made him forget the cave and his promise to Falak. But Falak's cave in the mountain is always there, and if you close your eyes tightly, you can go there, too. It's where we're all from, a place of endless calm and light. We just forget. Don't forget, Eivan."

Eivan was sucking his thumb now, his eyelids drooping then bobbing up as he fought against sleep. I wanted to slip into sleep with him. What I wouldn't do to be back in Kocho under my blanket, Hassan whistling as he fixed the wires on a broken radio, Adlan banging pots as she made kubbeh, and my sisters' breaths warm on my neck.

The floorboards in the hallway creaked suddenly.

Al-Amriki's guests were leaving.

A wave of terror moved through me.

"*As-salamu alaykum,*" I heard al-Amriki say.

"*Wa alaykumu s-salam,*" said another man.

Arabic was a language that had once reminded me of a love poem. I hated the sound of it now.

"Eivan," I said quickly, jolting him from his slumber. He wiped his face and stared up at me. "I want you to always remember that place up in the caves. Think of it now: that safe place that is only full of love. Think of your mother and Fallah, your father. Think of all the things that make you happy. This is part of the game I told you about. Remember? When you are calm and still, even when there is a lot of noise around you, you'll be guided to a safe place. Be calm by remembering your mother's kisses and your father's hugs."

Eivan nodded as al-Amriki pushed open the kitchen door.

Eivan screamed.

Al-Amriki slapped him across the face.

Then he moved toward me. He reached out and grabbed my hair and started dragging me along the floor. I winced from the pain. Then suddenly, I was no longer there. I was floating up toward the clouds, holding Eivan and Adlan's hands.

I heard someone screaming, and for a fleeting moment, I knew it was me. But she was very far away as I slipped up into the cave of white light and pretty music where Falak granted immortality.

Chapter Fifteen

Jinn

It was after my grandmother died that I began to see *jinn*.

At first, I told no one.

One of the jinn was an old man. He never allowed me to see his face full-on. He'd always talk to me in profile. He wore black clothes, and he was dark skinned, that much I could tell. He wasn't very tall. But he wasn't short either.

There were more of them, younger men, one of which was not much older than a boy.

Jinn, my mother had told me when I was little, were made from fire. They were part spirit, part human, able to possess people and trick them. Jinn live in the shadows in dark, dank places.

Jinn could be either good or bad. The jinn I saw weren't nice. They would tell me I was dirty. They would order me to laugh or cry on the spot, punching me if I refused their demands. They would scream at me to throw my plate of food to the floor. I did it because, otherwise, they threatened to beat my legs and back with sticks. Adlan got cross with me for breaking so many dishes. The jinn would tail me as I walked to and from school. They'd hide behind trees and throw bruised apples at my legs. They took my shampoo and hid it right when I needed it.

They warned me that if I told anyone about them, I would be sorry.

But one day, when they were right on my heels as I came home from the shops and the old man jinni was blathering about how ugly I was, I decided I'd had enough. I marched right into our house and got my brother Fallah, who was back in Kocho from his police job in Shingal preparing for his wedding. I took him outside, into a grove of Dake's fruit trees, and pointed to the jinn. They were laughing and pointing back at us.

Fallah scratched his head and then looked at me questioningly. "I can't see anything, Badeeah," he said, drawing out the syllables in my name. "Are you sure this isn't just your imagination? You fell very ill after Dake died. Maybe you're still suffering from fever?"

The old man jinni hacked the back of my legs with a wet towel. I screamed. But Fallah didn't see a thing. Instead, he laughed and said I should go see Bahar. Bahar was a local woman who could speak to the spirit world.

Bahar received me in a shed attached to her house. Once inside, I sat on a pillow on her Turkish carpet while she explained that my problem was difficult. Taking away spirits was challenging. I would have to visit her once a week for a month.

My father agreed to pay for my sessions with Bahar. She told me to make squiggly lines and diagrams on paper that she then had me burn. I had to recite phrases in a language I'd never heard before. Bahar said she was connecting to the jinn world through what I was doing, asking the jinn to leave.

In my last session with Bahar, she went into some kind of trance. When she emerged, she looked at me with cloudy eyes.

"Two hundred years ago, a Yazidi man named Mam Isso predicted there would be bad times coming for us," she said. Her hands shook as she spoke. "He said the whole world would hear about the Yazidi through Kocho. Everyone was surprised he would say such a thing. At that time, because of the genocides, the Kocho villagers had dispersed and were living close to Shingal. I am seeing this man now." Her words made me shudder.

"I don't know why," she continued. "But I hear him now, giving this warning again."

I was too shocked to believe her. Fallah had to be right. His explanation that jinn weren't real, that they were just in my imagination, made more sense. From that day on, I never saw the jinn again.

But in Aleppo that morning, just before I came to in the foggy place between sleep and wakefulness, I saw the old man jinni. "We finally have you," he gloated. "We have you in our lair."

∾

I sat up with a jolt.

Breathing heavily, I looked around. The jinni had disappeared.

I was lying on a floor with a cream-colored carpet. A rumpled, bloodied white sheet was wrapped around my legs. The room smelled of deodorant and mildew.

I rolled onto my side and threw up. With every heave, pain pulsed through me.

As my body started to relax, I saw the bruises on my wrists and ankles. I touched my cheeks. The skin where al-Amriki had slapped me was rough and raw. I groaned as I tried to stand.

My clothes were strewn around the room. I put them on slowly, breathing deeply, in an attempt to lessen the pain shooting through me.

The door was slightly ajar, and I could hear al-Amriki in another part of the house murmuring his prayers. I wanted to be dressed and back in the kitchen by the time he was done. I wanted to get as far away as possible from this man.

And then I remembered that he had threatened me with a gun. My eyes darted around the room, looking for the weapon. But everything, including the Quran and prayer beads he had laid out the night before, was gone. My heart sank. I'd had a vision where I saw myself grabbing his weapon, filling the chamber with bullets, the way I had seen Hassan fill his, and shooting al-Amriki.

I had always avoided the men's talk of war and murder. I wanted to be a doctor, to save lives. Now something new and terrible flowed through me: an anger so strong I could kill. I saw myself, for the first time ever, taking someone else's life. I had opened the door to hate.

I was putting on my headscarf when al-Amriki came to tell me he was leaving. He would be home at nightfall, he said, and he was stationing a guard in the house to keep an eye on us.

I was to teach Navine the Fatiha, the opening of the Quran, he said. At midday, the guard would show us how to pray.

"What about the others?" I asked.

"They're gone," he said with a wicked smile.

"What?"

"This morning. I sold them. All of them, except the boy. The remaining girl, Navine, she's a gift for a friend. She stays until he gets back."

Al-Amriki grunted as he strapped on the ammunition belt he was carrying. His bare feet made slapping sounds on the wooden tiles.

When I heard the front door open and then close, I bent at the waist and vomited again.

∽

"We need to escape," I told Navine that morning. The house was silent except for an occasional cough from the guard and the dripping of the showerhead. Eivan was playing with his taxi while Navine and I huddled in close together. A few times, I thought I could hear the old man jinni laughing.

Navine shook her head. "He'll kill us if we try to leave," she said. "And where would we go? How would we get out of Aleppo? We don't even know how to find Iraq from here."

In Raqqa, Navine had been the confident, strong one, the one not afraid of death. Now it was me.

"The translator said to ask if we needed anything, and he or a guard would get it. I'll say we need things . . ."

"More rice," Navine suggested, her shoulders lifting. She slid over on her knees to show me the bag. It was half full, but she got up and poured some of the rice down the sink. That way, when the guard looked, the bag would be nearly empty.

"When the guard leaves for the market," I continued, "we'll go, too, but in the opposite direction."

We would have to leave in the clothes we were wearing despite the chill in the air. I wanted to find something warm for Eivan, though. In the room where Navine had slept, I spied a small pink coat and grabbed it. One of the other mothers must have left it behind. Navine discovered two khimars in the closet. The capelike garments would shield us a bit from the cold.

Summoning up my courage, I told the guard what we needed: rice and tomatoes, as well as some shampoo and some medicine for Eivan. The more items he had to collect, the longer he would be gone, I hoped.

We held our breath as the front door and then the wrought-iron gate creaked open and closed again. The guard hadn't locked either of them. He must have been confident we would be too afraid to escape.

Quickly, Navine and I wrapped the khimars around us. At the front door, we found our shoes and I put the pink coat on Eivan.

Outside, the cool air hit me hard. Autumn was well underway. Back in Kocho, we'd have been met with the scent of smoky chimney fires, wet leaves, and the rich aromas of cinnamon and roasted fruits from Adlan's jam making.

I cautiously poked my head out of the gate and caught sight of the guard disappearing into a store. I pulled Navine and Eivan in the opposite direction toward the building where I had seen the woman on the balcony.

My heart beat fast as we ran down an alleyway.

With every step, pain from al-Amriki's assault spiked through me. But we had to press on. This might be our only chance to get away.

As we rounded a bend, I stopped dead in my tracks, pulling Navine and Eivan in behind me.

A woman was swaying down the alley ahead of us. She carried a large tray covered in tea towels, and I could smell fresh-baked bread and savory spices. She didn't notice us at first, but when she realized she was no longer alone, she turned, looking startled, and asked us what we wanted.

My mouth was dry, and I fumbled to find the words. Before I could speak, a door slid open and a tall, older man in a dishdasha emerged.

"Who are you?" he demanded. The woman slipped in behind him and disappeared.

"We need a hospital," I managed to get out.

"Why?" he said with a snarl.

My heart raced, and my head spun. The man crossed his arms and tapped his foot.

"My sister is pregnant," I finally spluttered. "She needs a woman to help as she's in pain." I thought hard. "Her husband is gone to Dayr Hafir. There is something wrong with the baby."

The woman who had been carrying the food reappeared. Up close, her face looked younger than her humped frame would suggest. Her eyes were lined in dark kohl that made them look hauntingly yellow, like snakeskins.

"Take care of these two," the man hissed at her.

The woman glared at us before grumbling that we should follow her.

"You're having a baby?" she asked Navine as we moved back down the road toward al-Amriki's house. Suddenly, I was very afraid.

"Yes," I replied. "My sister is so distressed she can't speak."

"We need to get off the street," the woman said, speeding up. "The Adhan will sound soon. You can't be outside during prayers."

We were now back on the main road. I wrapped the khimar around my face so that only my eyes were showing and nudged Navine to do the same.

"They round up anyone who is on the streets during prayers and imprison and torture them. One time, a woman went out without her khimar. Daesh killed her husband and put her in prison," the woman elaborated. "We can't go to the hospital until prayers are finished."

The woman turned into a courtyard, and the house she led us into was low, bungalow style, with a partial second floor in the back. The place was eerily quiet.

When the woman took off her khimar and niqab, her silky dark hair reminded me of Hadil's and Majida's. She gestured for Navine and me to remove our outer clothes as well.

I took a deep breath. "Please," I said, "you need to help us. Just lend us a phone . . . anything . . . to get us out of here. We will give you money, lots of it."

The woman's eyes grew wide. "She's not pregnant, then?" She pointed at Navine.

I shook my head. "We've been kidnapped." I reached out and clasped her arm. "We were taken from our village in Iraq. Our mothers and fathers are looking for us. We have to go home. Whatever you want, I will find a way to reward you."

The woman spoke sharply. "That building where the man talked to you? It's Daesh's office. You don't know what you are asking me!"

I fell to my knees. "Please," I begged. "You're a woman. You must understand." Eivan, seeing my distress, began to whimper. He scrambled out of Navine's arms and threw himself against me.

The woman motioned for me to stand up. "You need to leave when prayers are over," she said, looking away.

I started to sob. The woman turned and went into another room where we could hear her saying her prayers.

When she returned, she put on her khimar and niqab set. "Wait here," she said, her voice sounding much kinder. "I'll see what I can do."

For half an hour, I paced, Eivan on my heels, Navine wringing her hands and jumping at every sound from outside.

When we finally heard a key in the lock, all three of us stood up straight. The floor underneath us fell away as al-Amriki entered the room. I heard the old man jinni laughing again. We were trapped.

∾

Al-Amriki drove us to a building a few miles away. He was taking us to the courthouse, he said, where judges would decide whether we should be sent to prison or executed.

Behind a long table in a big room sat three men. The bearded man in the middle, who seemed to be in charge, asked over and over again in Arabic why we had run away. He quoted the *hadith*—instructions from the prophet Muhammad—on the role of women obeying their husbands, including not leaving the house without the man's permission.

"I thought my son was very ill. It was an emergency. I had no choice but to leave the house," I pleaded. "That woman is the liar! I wanted a hospital for my son."

Navine joined in, speaking in Shingali. The main judge frowned. Finally, he raised his large hands, bellowed for Navine to stop talking, and ordered me to translate what she had said. I knew some Islamic law from school. "In the Quran, is it not permissible for a wife to leave her house without her husband's consent if it is an emergency?

She is telling you that my son is sick. We were looking for medicine."

The judge motioned for a small, thin man to approach me. In his hand, he held a leather-bound copy of the Quran. "Hold your right hand on the Quran and say three times that you were not running away," the main judge told me.

I stared at the book, unable to move. Out of the corner of my eye, I could see al-Amriki lean forward, his piercing eyes following my every move.

I swallowed hard. Guilt moved through me. It was one thing to tell small lies to save us. This would be lying to God. I thought of Lalish and our temples, our gentle faith that encourages tolerance and love, and the mysticism that moves through me—but that has been the source of our persecution for centuries. I was proud to be Yazidi. I was about to answer that I would never abandon my faith when I heard my mother's voice. "Do it. If you don't, you might lose Eivan." My mother was right. The Islam this man and the other Daesh jihadis practiced was no religion in my books. I was sure Allah would forgive me.

"Swear on the Quran you were not running away," the main judge said again in a loud voice.

The spindly man held the Quran up in front of me. I put my right hand on the book. "I swear by Allah, I was not running away," I said. "I was asking the woman for help to find medicine and for a hospital for my son."

The judge may have believed me, but al-Amriki didn't. Back at his house, he beat Navine and me. He kicked us both in the rib cage. Slapped our cheeks. Spat in our faces.

When he finally left the house, he locked us inside with a guard and took a squealing Eivan with him.

Chapter Sixteen

Death

When al-Amriki returned, he announced that he had sold Eivan.

I wailed as if I were at a funeral, rolling on the kitchen floor and digging my nails into my legs until I bled. I pulled out chunks of my hair.

But al-Amriki didn't care.

That night, when he ordered me to bathe before going to his room, I clutched his legs tight. "Please," I begged. "Please bring my son back. I will do whatever you say. I will be your bride forever."

"You can fool the judge, but you can't fool me," al-Amriki snarled.

I let go of him and leapt to my feet. I started bowing, raising my arms and lowering them the way Daesh did in Muslim prayer. As I did so, I recalled aloud some things I knew from overhearing the Muslim men who visited my father: "Allah does not love the oppressor. You holding us here is like oppression. Allah will be angry with you."

Al-Amriki just stared at me.

"As I am your wife, my son and any children I have and any nieces or nephews are part of the family, too."

Al-Amriki shook his head and pushed me away from him. "In ten minutes, I will watch you bathe. Ten minutes. Be in the shower room."

I listened as a closet door opened in the hallway and al-Amriki rummaged around. He returned to the kitchen with some goat meat, enough for one person. He ordered Navine to start cooking it. When he was done with me, he said, he would eat.

"There is something you can do," he said to me as he turned to leave.

"Anything to get my son back," I promised. "Anything you ask."

"Start praying," he grunted. "Pray tonight. And tomorrow, five times a day. And teach her," he said, waving a hand at Navine. "You will soon learn that Islam is the way. Yours is a false God."

The days that followed passed slowly, like melting ice. Navine did all the cooking because I had no energy to help. I sat silently, my back up against the wall.

I heard the voices of men coming and going as they met with al-Amriki. Navine made them their Lipton tea and served them nuts, figs, and candies that al-Amriki hid in another part of the house.

When the sound of the Adhan from a nearby mosque floated through the kitchen, I stood, motioning for Navine to follow me. As I recited the Muslim prayers, I thought about Khatuna Fakhra. I wanted to reach out to her, but I felt she had abandoned me. I had been tricked at Raqqa when I was reunited with Eivan. Now Eivan was gone for good. I had failed him. I had failed my family.

I thought of ways to kill myself. Once, in Kocho, a young man had shown up at the doctor's with a wound to his neck. The man had bled out before the doctor could see him. If I could hang onto a sharp knife after the cooking was done, I could stab myself. But a guard always collected the knife once Navine was through with it.

I fingered the hijab I wore except when I was alone with al-Amriki. Maybe I could hang myself from the shower curtain rod. One afternoon, while al-Amriki was away, I hurried to the shower room, but Navine was right behind me. She had guessed that I wanted to harm myself, and she wasn't going to give me the chance.

∽

I seemed trapped in a time that was bleak and endless.

It was November, I estimated, maybe December. That meant we'd been in captivity for nearly four months.

I stopped fighting al-Amriki. Whenever he wanted me, I went without a struggle. Whenever I mentioned Eivan's name, though, al-Amriki insisted he had been sold.

At Navine's urging, I resumed helping her make food for the men who visited. As I placed the trays by the door of the guest room, I tried to overhear their conversations.

One time, I heard the men speaking about new recruits. Apparently, ten foreigners—a few from Germany, some from Great Britain—had just arrived in Aleppo and they were being interrogated to make sure they were not Western spies.

One of the men said the foreigners should be used to make propaganda videos to attract more Western Muslims to become part of the nation of Islam.

"You should be on camera, too," I heard the man say to al-Amriki. I could tell from his voice that the man was young, maybe just a teenager.

Al-Amriki was his usual belligerent self, yelling that he would never be photographed. Another man agreed, asserting that al-Amriki was too high up to have his picture taken, that it would draw the attention of the Americans, who would then want to hunt him down.

The following day, the men left the door to the room wide open. I could see them looking at a map pinned up on the wall. Al-Amriki held a pointing stick, and he was issuing instructions. When he was finished, he took the map down and tucked it in the sofa.

One afternoon, when al-Amriki was gone, I pulled the map out from its hiding place. But I was too afraid to open it because a guard was nearby.

On other days, a Daesh soldier would arrive with a long box. Al-Amriki would open the box and pull out a weapon. Usually, they were AK-47s, but sometimes they were shoulder-held missiles. Every day, it seemed, a new weapon was delivered for our captor to examine and explain to the others. I gathered from the conversations that it was his decision whether or not Daesh would invest in the weapon.

Eavesdropping on the men gave me something to do. I had nothing left inside me with Eivan gone. I had no hope of leaving this city, where even the women had been brainwashed to abuse other women and girls. I fought crippling fatigue and increasing thoughts of suicide. But I had to listen because I had fleeting thoughts of finding a way to tell the Peshmerga or the Americans what Daesh was doing. If I could get them the map somehow, my death would be worth it.

I also memorized passages from the Quran to use on al-Amriki. "Allah is ever pardoning and all powerful," I said to him one night. "If Allah can forgive, so can you. Please forgive me and bring Eivan back."

Al-Amriki didn't sleep much. He'd pace and talk on his phone and his computer, speaking loudly as if the whole world were awake with him. I would lie motionless after his abuse and listen to his conversations. Often, I'd hear a woman's voice on the other end. A few times, when he thought I was sleeping, al-Amriki set up his computer in the corner of the room. Then I could see her, the woman he spoke to. Her hair was the color of straw. She sometimes wore a headscarf, but it was tied loosely, so strands of her hair fell onto her face.

The way he spoke to her was gentle and soft, like she was his real wife.

I was heartsick. What little I knew about love and marriage was now muddled with additional wives and wives that were spoils of war. Some Yazidi men had more than one wife. But my father and older brothers had shown me, through their love for my mother and their wives, what a marriage was supposed to be. Their marriages were built on respect, loyalty, kindness, and an honoring of each other's strengths. Marriage in my culture was a bond celebrated with rituals and a ceremony, not just a man saying, "I take you as my wife."

On the night of day nine without Eivan, some Daesh soldiers arrived to tell al-Amriki that we had to leave for another location. As I set out the trays of tea, Turkish pastries, olives, and cheese, I overheard that our move would be at midnight. "In the dead of the night, when nothing moves," said one of the men in a deep squawk.

Other voices explained that airplanes were coming.

Despite the hope that some army might be looking for us, a dark shadow passed over me. Moving meant even if we could escape, I would never be able to find Eivan. At least from this house, I had a starting point.

Back in the kitchen, I studied the electrical socket the fridge was plugged into. It gave me an idea. I decided I'd start washing dishes at the time I knew the men would want refills of their tea. I'd ask Navine to serve them. With her gone, even if only for a few seconds, I'd stick a piece of cutlery into the socket with my wet fingers.

But on that evening, a guard didn't come to say the men wanted refills. Instead, he ordered us to help al-Amriki pack. We couldn't wait until midnight to leave, he said. Dusk had cloaked the city. We had to go now.

Chapter Seventeen

Houses

I was ordered to put al-Amriki's clothes in boxes while he packed his computers. He had a stash of phones, too, along with radios, guns, and ammunition that two guards loaded into a waiting truck. When we were ready to go, I begged al-Amriki to let me take one item: the pink little girl's coat. It reminded me of Eivan. It was my last piece of him.

We got into a minivan, with al-Amriki climbing into the front seat beside the driver. Navine and I sat together behind the men, clutching each other's hands under our khimars.

Behind and in front of us were pickup trucks filled with weapons and heavily armed soldiers.

As we crept through Aleppo's haunted streets, I could see the silhouettes of unlit apartment buildings. Aleppo, like Kocho, seemed to have power for only a few hours a day. Light from candles or kerosene lamps flickered from some of the windows.

Overhead, the sky was clear. There were occasional flashes of light, which I knew must come from bombs or heavy fighting in another part of the city.

The house we headed to was not far away. The courtyard was filled with potholes and weeds. The front door, made of flimsy wood, had a dent that looked as if it had been made by a fist.

I choked on the air inside the house: stale but with an overlay of something else. Like a dead dog. I breathed into my hijab.

Al-Amriki was shaking his head and talking wildly in English to another Daesh man. I didn't need to know English to understand the house was no good. A few Arabic words were thrown around, too: the house smelled of *almawt:* "death." It was *muqassis:* "disgusting." It dawned on me that Daesh was taking over the homes of dead people or refugees who had fled.

Back in the car, al-Amriki rolled the back windows down partway so that we could breathe in the fresher night air. We didn't drive off right away.

"Important man . . . the house is for the Sheikh of Aleppo," the guard in the driver's seat yelled into his phone.

We drove farther this time along streets lined with tall, ornate buildings. They, too, were dark, creeping with ghosts that made my skin crawl.

As we passed abandoned churches and mosques, I gazed at the buildings. For some strange reason, they comforted me. The crosses and minarets on top were like beacons, reminding all of us that Aleppo was better than its Daesh invaders. For the first time since Eivan was taken, I felt a stirring of hope.

Finally, the driver stopped in front of a two-story house. From the outside, it looked like a small, stone palace. Inside, though, the paint was peeling, the ceramic tiles were cracked, and the ceiling was falling down in places. This was a house of war, I could see. In the main room, the scent of soldiers still lingered. In the kitchen, ashtrays overflowed with cigarette butts. Tea glasses had been abandoned, some half full. Pots with burnt rice stuck to them had been left in the sink.

Despite the hour, al-Amriki ordered Navine and me to start cleaning. He liked things neat. Even his room, with his few belongings, was always carefully arranged.

But after our khimars were off, al-Amriki changed his mind.

"I want to go to sleep," he said, nodding at me. "Clean yourself and come with me."

He ordered Navine to accompany me to bathe while he took another phone call.

I let Navine lift up my dress and peel down my pants. There was no bathtub in the room, just a small shower with white tiles. The shower curtain was a pale yellow, hanging from a thin metal rod that I was sure would never hold my weight. A bright bulb dangled from the ceiling. That's how I could do it: stick a metal spoon into that socket.

"I need to tell you something," I said to Navine as the room filled up with steam.

She turned to face me.

"I'm lost without Eivan. I don't want to live anymore."

Navine leaned back against the door. "We will find Eivan. You have to trust."

"No, we won't." My face burned. My chest felt tight. "The soldier al-Amriki wants to give you to will be coming soon. As soon as al-Amriki leaves for his next mission, you need to leave me alone long enough for me to die. Then find me, cause a commotion, and while the guard is trying to revive me, you slip out. Don't ask anyone for help this time. Keep running, hiding, until you are out of this city—"

"I won't go without you," she cut in.

"I can't face my family ever again," I murmured. "I've lost everything."

Al-Amriki's voice rose and fell like the waves of the sea. He was in a nearby room talking in English.

"Get in," Navine said, flicking her head toward the shower. When I was standing under the weak current, the water smelling of rotting garbage, Navine pulled the plastic shower curtain around me.

∽

Usually, whenever al-Amriki took me to his room, he would attack me right away. On this night, though, he wanted to talk. Unlike the last house, this room had a bed with a box spring and mattress. He gestured for me to sit on top of it.

"I was not happy in the United States," he started, leaning back on his arm. "Something was missing. I traveled to Syria and met people who explained Islam in a way I'd never known before. I went back to my country and started studying the Quran. I found Allah. I decided to return to Syria and become a Muslim. Then I found the way." After a brief pause, he continued speaking. "My Syrian friends called me to say they were creating a worldwide caliphate, and they asked me to join them. Of course, I did. I wanted to join the Islamic State, and I want everyone to know Allah."

"You're a son of a bitch," I said in Shingali. I smiled as I said it, so al-Amriki would think I was agreeing with him.

"We have so much suffering in the world," he said, letting the curtain fall and looking around the room dreamily. "I don't mean just poverty and wars. I mean the hate and greed that have become addictions. Especially in America, people are jealous and godless. I want to represent Allah to the whole world. You understand?"

I ground my teeth. Of course, I understood. I understood he was an egomaniac. "Yes, son of a bitch," I replied again in Shingali.

Adlan, I wanted to tell him, had said to me once that the greatest misunderstanding is people's belief that only what they can see is real. "What we imagine, we create," she had told me. "We stop giving birth to beauty when we believe only the eyes have vision." She had pointed a spot on her forehead, the spot where she said the mystics heard their celestial sounds. "What's in there is real. That's the place where love enters. If you create your world from that place, you create happiness."

". . . the poor getting poorer, the rich and powerful doing whatever they want," al-Amriki was saying. "I hate my president." He clenched his fists. "President Obama. If I ever got the chance, I would behead him. I hate America, and I hate everything American. Our leaders lie through their teeth, and the people just buy it."

A fury bubbling deep inside me started to rise. I didn't care that the American army might still be looking for us or that the helicopters and airplanes I heard in the distance might be them trying to end this war. No. I was angry at America: a nation that had so much but still created animals like al-Amriki.

"Who is the crazy one?" I asked al-Amriki in Shingali.

"Could you speak in Arabic?" he said, calmly for once.

I switched to Arabic. "Now that you are here, you have a choice not to do what you are doing. You have a choice not to oppress others. You have a choice not to kill people weaker than you. You have a choice to not take girls and women against their will."

"We didn't destroy your village," he said defensively. "That was Daesh in Iraq."

I looked at him straight on, something I had never done before, and continued. "We had a Yazidi female leader, Mayan Khatun, who realized that our oppression at the hands of our enemies had led us to oppress our own families. The regent said the Yazidi could not advance until the family and the balance of respect between males and females was restored. I don't know a lot about Islam, but I am sure Allah is about love and respect, too. You've got it wrong."

Al-Amriki breathed heavily. "Who are you? A spy? Why are you saying such things?"

I was sure he was going to beat me for talking back. But I didn't look away or brace myself. For the first time with him, I experienced my power. Under my gaze, he seemed to cower, and I saw him as a lost little boy. What al-Amriki didn't know was that I now had control. I didn't care whether I lived or died.

There was a knock on the front door followed by a male voice calling, "Sheikh."

Al-Amriki jumped up and left the room.

Moments later, he called out for me.

Halfway down the corridor, I stopped. I smelled peppermint and then caramel. I heard the unmistakable sound of crinkling candy wrappers.

My breathing grew labored, and my heart fluttered.

"Mama," I heard a soft voice call. "Mama?"

I rushed to the front hallway to see Eivan standing beside al-Amriki. His hands were full of candies, and his mouth was covered in chocolate.

"I brought him back for you," al-Amriki said.

Eivan ran to me, touching my face with his sticky hands.

Light had returned to my darkness.

Chapter Eighteen

Reunion

"A horrible witch. Not like Falak in the story," Eivan was telling me. "This witch made me sweep her house and all of outside."

Al-Amriki had sold him to a fat old woman who treated him like a slave, according to Eivan.

It was the middle of the night. Al-Amriki had allowed me to sleep with Eivan in Navine's room. Tomorrow I would have to go back to him.

Navine was sound asleep. The three of us were in a child's bed—barely enough space for one person—on a foam mattress and with one rough wool blanket for us all to share. Our bodies molded together kept us warm.

The house was quiet except for the *drip, drip* of water from the leaky showerhead and Eivan recounting his tale. "She had black warts on her face and smelled like she never bathed. I had to get a bucket of water and soap and scrub the stones."

"What did you eat?" I asked. After the initial shock of having Eivan returned, I noticed that he had shrunk. His pants slipped down when he walked. His rib cage jutted out underneath skin that was yellow from the lack of vitamins and proper nutrition. Even his chubby cheeks had wilted.

"She gave me an onion to eat," he said, pretending to spit. "She hit me when I was hungry and asked for more."

I winced. I was grateful there was no light. I didn't want Eivan to see the horror on my face.

"But when the evil witch hit me, I didn't cry," Eivan said with pride. I bit the flesh inside my cheek to stop myself from weeping. "I wasn't going to be like Mir Meh. I remembered you and Mama," he whispered in my ear.

Once he finally fell asleep, I lay on my back reciting the numbers Salwa had given me in my head: the phone number for our cousin Ameen.

∾

I did everything I had promised al-Amriki I would do if he returned Eivan. I made his meals. I helped Navine clean.

When al-Amriki was not at home, I continued to read the Quran. As I mulled over various passages, the anger inside me grew stronger. Al-Amriki had a very narrow reading of his holy book. He picked only the verses, sometimes parts of verses, that supported his selfish needs. I said nothing to him, fearing he would take Eivan again. But words were steaming inside me, ready to explode.

Day by day, the bombs and whirring helicopters crept closer. War was coming to us. I didn't need to listen in on al-Amriki and his soldiers to know that.

One evening, after the men visiting him had left the house, al-Amriki made me come and sit beside him.

His laptop computer was open on his lap. On the screen was the blonde woman.

I kept my eyes lowered, having no idea how one wife was supposed to treat another, if she was indeed his wife. I'd never spoken to a Western woman before.

The blonde woman said something in English.

"Look at her," Al-Amriki snapped at me.

I looked up. The woman was speaking to me, it seemed, but I couldn't understand her. She wasn't wearing a head covering, and her hair fell straight and thin to her shoulders. She had a long, oval face with high cheekbones, but she wasn't beautiful. There was something severe about her. Even though she parted her thin lips in a smile, I couldn't help but shudder, feeling she was full of hate.

I heard a baby cooing in the background. The woman shifted her body, disappeared from the screen, and then reappeared with a baby boy in her arms. He was maybe a year old.

The child had a shiny, bald head and pink, glowing skin. The woman poked her head out from behind the child and said more words in English as the boy blew air bubbles.

I started to knot the bottom of my dress and then untie it again. We were rotting away here, but this boy wasn't just healthy, he was robust.

Al-Amriki had enslaved a child only a few years older than his own, I wanted to scream to this woman. Did she know that? Did she even care? What kind of woman was she?

Then, they were gone. The electricity in the house flickered on and off until it finally went out altogether.

That night, al-Amriki told me he had to go to Kobani, in northern Syria, for several days. There were problems, I could hear it in his voice, maybe more than he'd experienced before. Kobani, which al-Amriki boasted belonged to Daesh, was under attack. He would be leaving in the morning. He said that when he returned, he would take Navine as his second wife. His friend was not coming after all.

I protested on Navine's behalf, saying that al-Amriki needed a slave, a cook, and a cleaner. He already had two wives. "I am your main wife," I said to him. "I'm with you all the time. I won't let you take another wife. It's not right."

"It's okay," he said. "If you stay here with me, we'll have a nice life. I won't sell you to anyone else."

What he didn't know was that I would never allow Navine to be hurt the way I was. I would find a way to kill him before it came to that.

"You've proven that I can trust you," he continued. "I need all my guards to fight. I will lock you in the house with enough food when I go, but you'll be alone."

A wave of excitement pulsed through me. This time, I would find a phone and call Ameen. I would not wait for someone from Aleppo to help me.

"Besides," he said, his voice drifting into sleep, "you won't escape. I've heard that Yazidi girls like you, who have been married to Daesh men, are killed when they return to their people. Your own people don't want you back."

My pulse quickened. A heavy weight bore down on me. "What?"

"Yazidi men are killing their women," he said. "Fathers are killing their own daughters."

"I don't understand."

Al-Amriki was asleep. But my own eyes would not shut.

All that night, my thoughts tumbled and crashed into each another. I knew that the Yazidi were strict with their daughters. A few girls had even been murdered for falling in love with non-Yazidi boys. When I asked my mother why, she said the Yazidi control of girls was a dark shadow.

"Badeeah, our evolution is like an ocean tide. We progress, then retreat into our fears. This is what Mayan Khatun witnessed when the Yazidi were under Ottoman control. Men, alienated from themselves, living in fear and anger, in turn oppress those closest to them. Cities, cultures, religions, and people are the same. Until we're whole, we move backward and forward."

What if al-Amriki was telling the truth? What if our brothers and fathers, after years of being held down by Saddam Hussein and now Daesh, were killing us? What if I managed to make it back to Iraq with Eivan only to face my own death?

Chapter Nineteen

Escape

"Let's go now," Navine urged, snapping her fingers as I wiped Eivan's face with the back of my sleeve.

Before leaving for the battle in Kobani, one of the house guards had fetched enough food for us from the market for three days. Eivan was shoving the rice I'd mashed with roasted tomatoes and eggplant into his mouth. When his plate was licked clean, he begged for more.

"You can't eat too much," I explained, "or you'll get sick. I know you're starving, Eivan." I crouched down beside him. "But this is our chance to escape. You've been so good with our games so far. Can you be quiet for a little longer and just follow my orders?"

Eivan nodded.

"Go to the front of the house with Navine," I said, forcing a smile as I helped him into the pink coat. "I'll be right behind you."

I grabbed my khimar, but instead of swaddling my body in it, I headed to al-Amriki's room. My heart racing, I ran to the secret cupboard where he sometimes locked away his food, radios, guns, and, I hoped, his maps. It was locked. I kicked the door. I threw a chair against it over and over again, but the wood would not splinter. Frantically, I began pulling apart the cushions in the guest room. Nothing. I ran back to his bedroom and pulled apart his bedding, hurling it across the room. No maps, but underneath the mattress, I found his phone, the fancy one that looked like a small television.

I hurried to the front of the house. "How do you use this?" I asked, thrusting the phone toward Navine.

We punched buttons on the screen. Some pictures of al-Amriki's American wife and son popped up. But we couldn't get it to work as a telephone. The only phones we'd ever used were Nokias. Frustrated, I slipped the phone into my pocket. If we managed to get out of Aleppo, I could give it to the Peshmerga or the American army. Maybe al-Amriki also stored important Daesh information on it.

I put a niqab on and wrapped the khimar around me. "Okay, let's go. We'll have to find another phone."

Navine had discovered a hammer buried under the cleaning supplies in the kitchen. She pounded at the lock on the front door until eventually it yielded. She turned the knob, and together the three of us stepped outside.

∽

My eyes squinted against the winter sun. It was a bright, cloudless day. I could see my breath in the air.

I squeezed Eivan's hand tight to steady my nerves.

We moved at a rapid pace down the street, hoping we looked like Muslim wives out shopping. We rounded one corner and then another, unsure of where we were going.

I looked down at Eivan. I could tell from his tense expression that he was scared, but he was doing what I had instructed him to do. His bravery touched me.

I trembled as we fell in behind a woman carrying a black plastic shopping bag.

Soon I heard the din of a market: buyers and sellers heckling over prices, people shouting, and babies crying.

Despite the cool weather, I was perspiring under the weight of the khimar by the time we made it to the market. I knew we would be punished severely if we were discovered escaping a second time. I might even face the death penalty for lying under oath on the Quran.

"Over there," Navine said, spinning my body around. I peered through the small crowd of shoppers, mostly other women in black khimars.

A nearby display case held electronic devices, including fancy cell phones like al-Amriki's.

Navine pulled me toward the shop.

The older man behind the counter had a well-weathered face, and his black beard was short, not long like those of the Daesh men.

"What can I do for you?" the man asked. His voice was husky, as if he'd spent a lifetime smoking. Fighting every instinct to run away, I glanced at the display. I wondered if I should give him al-Amriki's phone and ask him how to use it. Just as I was about to do so, I spied Nokia phones sitting in a bowl on top of the display case.

I swallowed. "We just need to make one call, on one of these," I said to the man, pointing to the Nokia phones.

The man did not reply. His silence felt like a knife stabbing me. He was going to call Daesh and send us back to al-Amriki; I was sure of it. The man's slender hands shook as he reached into the front pocket of his apron.

I kept talking. "My father left for Dayr Hafir," I said. "He forgot to give my sister and me money for food. I need to call a relative to give us money." As I spoke, I ran Ameen's phone number over and over again in my head so I wouldn't forget it. "I can't pay you, not now," I told the man. "But if you can let us make this call, I will bring you some money. Please help us."

If the man pulled out a gun, I told myself, I would step in front of Navine and Eivan to take the bullet. But when his shaky hand emerged from his apron pocket, he was holding a cell phone.

"Tell me the number," he said, his eyes darting around the market. I realized then that he was just as afraid as we were.

As I whispered the number, he punched it into his phone. At the market stall beside us, a younger man, short and stocky, hawked lemons, oranges, and pomegranate juice.

"Here," the older man said. I took the cell phone and a man's voice came through the receiver.

"Who is this?" the voice asked in Shingali.

Tears fell, soaking my khimar.

"Badeeah Hassan Ahmed," I said.

"Where are you?" he asked, breathing hard on the other end of the line. I didn't need to tell him why I was calling. He already knew.

"Aleppo."

"But where?"

Life drained out of me. I hadn't thought about that. I didn't know the address.

I looked up at the market seller. "Please," I stammered, "my sister, my son . . . we're from Turkey. I don't know the address where we're staying, and I need to give it to my relative so he can bring us money. Can you help?"

Another thick silence moved between us, drowning out the sounds of the market. For sure, I thought, this time we were dead.

"Tell the person you will call them back," the seller finally said.

I did what he asked. I had no choice.

"Take me to where you're staying," he said as he slipped on a jacket.

I couldn't breathe. What if this was a trap? What if this man knew al-Amriki? I suddenly thought I was going to pass out.

I felt Eivan tugging on my dress and glanced down into his sparkling eyes. I had to risk death to get him and Navine out of Aleppo.

"Follow me," I said to the market seller. "Follow me."

∾

Out on the street again, I jumped at the sound of a car engine backfiring.

As we turned the corner and al-Amriki's house came into view, I pulled Eivan in close to me.

When we were in front of the house, I pointed. "Here," I told the market seller.

The man took out his phone and redialed Ameen's number. After a short pause, he spoke the address of the house into the receiver, then passed me the phone.

"In a few hours," I heard Ameen say. My eyes remained glued to the market seller. I was searching for any sign that he was about to betray us. But he was watching a group of young men who were making their way toward us.

"Yes," I told my cousin. "In a few hours . . . what?"

"Get off the phone now," the market seller snapped at me.

"Someone named Nezar will come for you," Ameen said. "The password is his name. Do not open the door to anyone but him. Nezar is a human smuggler. He will get you out of Syria."

"Go inside the house," the market seller said sharply, his eyes still on the approaching youth. "It's not safe for you out here."

I hung up and gave the phone back.

"Thank you," I said to the market seller. "As-salamu alaykum." I bowed, then turned toward the house.

"Wait a minute," the seller said. He motioned for me to draw near. "You don't know me," he said in a low voice. "If you're caught, we never met. Promise me that?"

I nodded.

"And one other thing," he said, before waving me off. "These men who are imprisoning you, they're not Islam. When you're free, remember that we're still trapped in this city with them."

As soon as we stepped through the front door, I smelled al-Amriki. His sweat. His odor.

My body seized.

Navine came up behind me, loosened my khimar, and smoothed down my hair.

"He's not here," she reassured me, taking my hand and leading me to the kitchen. As she got me a drink of water, I slipped down onto the floor beside Eivan, who had dug out his toy taxi from its hiding place in a cupboard.

"Let me tell you another story," I said, struggling to stay calm as Eivan rolled the toy up my foot and down my leg.

"Once upon a time, there was a boy named Tasmasp who fell into a well after getting drowsy from eating too much honey. When he awoke at the bottom of the well, he was surrounded by snakes. One snake, who was named Samaran, had the head of a woman but the body of a reptile. Samaran took Tasmasp to her home deep under the ground, where she fed him dolma and kubbeh, all the foods he loved to eat."

Eivan smiled. He liked those foods, too.

"Samaran was very wise, and she told the boy stories about the history of humankind," I continued. "Then one day, she announced she had no more stories to tell. The young boy, now bored, wished to return to his parents. Samaran released him on one condition. He could not tell anyone where she lived. The boy agreed.

"Tasmasp grew into a man, and he kept his secret for many years. Then one day, the king of his country fell ill. The king called for Tasmasp and repeated a legend he had heard. If the king acquired the skin of Samaran, he would survive his illness and inherit all her wisdom. The king knew the boy had met Samaran, and he demanded to know where she could be found."

The Adhan sounded, announcing midday prayer.

"I'll tell you the ending when we reach Kocho," I said, stroking Eivan's forehead. "Because soon all of this will be over."

∽

"Wake up! Wake up!" I heard a voice say. I opened my eyes to see Navine. With a beaming smile, she passed me my khimar. "He's here," she said. "Your cousin's friend."

"How long did I sleep?" I asked.

"Nearly two hours," Navine said. "I didn't want to wake you. I knew you'd just be nervous waiting."

"Where's the man?"

"In the room where al-Amriki meets the other soldiers."

In the guest room, I faced a young man with a mustache dressed in a brown jacket and jeans. When he looked up at me, my knees buckled. He had big eyes that reminded me of my brother Fallah.

"Hello," he said in Shingali. "I'm Nezar."

∽

Nezar explained that we needed to walk out of the suburb where Daesh was keeping us toward east Aleppo, where he had parked his vehicle. We would pretend to be a Muslim family. We'd have to keep a brisk pace to get there before Asr, afternoon prayers.

Nezar's movements were hurried as he opened the front door. He checked in both directions, then waved us out onto the street. "Walk behind me," he ordered.

With every step, I cringed, expecting to be captured. With every step, I envisioned al-Amriki pulling up beside us in a white SUV. He'd shoot Nezar and take Eivan away, maybe this time making him one of their suicide bombers. Navine and I would surely be sentenced to death.

We passed khimar- and niqab-clad women on their way to visit friends, go to the bazaars, or run errands. Men smoked cigarettes. No one seemed to look our way.

At one point, a car horn blared, followed by men yelling and singing Daesh war songs. I glanced back to see a white Daesh truck creeping along behind us.

We were not going to make it.

We had been discovered.

Chapter Twenty

Return to Iraq

At the sound of gunshots, I braced myself.

The white truck was now beside us.

I kept my eyes lowered.

Men were shouting and firing their assault rifles into the air.

The truck moved in front of us. I swallowed hard as bile filled my throat.

And the truck moved away, turning off the road.

"Just some Daesh thugs. They're showing off," Nezar said over his shoulder when they were gone. But I could hear in his voice he had been afraid, too.

As we continued on, I was shocked at the carnage

around us: bombed-out buildings, boulder-sized chunks of cement. East Aleppo was the war zone, ground zero. The roads were full of rubble, carcasses of dead animals, children's toys, and women's scarves. Pages of discarded books flapped in the breeze. Nezar walked us carefully around a Daesh checkpoint monitored by several guards. I gritted my teeth, preparing to be discovered, but no one noticed us. The Daesh soldiers were too busy interrogating a family while war songs played from a car stereo.

An acrid smoke hung low around us: the charcoal remains of a once beautiful city.

∾

The Adhan announcing Asr blanketed the street just as we reached Nezar's car, a beat-up old black sedan he had parked on a side street.

Once we were settled in the car and driving, Nezar explained that we'd be traveling to a small outlying city, Manbij, about an hour and a half away.

We drove along grimy streets masked in soot. Dusk fell quickly at this time of year. But it was still light enough to see that every second house had been destroyed. Many of the houses still standing had been abandoned. Nezar explained that their former inhabitants had fled the country as refugees.

The civil war involved many combatants, Daesh being just one of them. "A war within a war," Nezar called it. The Arab Spring movement that had swept North Africa and the Middle East, toppling the Tunisian and Egyptian governments, had reached Syria in 2011. Protesters wanted more economic freedoms and liberties. But Syrian president Bashar al-Assad attempted to quash the revolt, killing and imprisoning hundreds of thousands of demonstrators. Defectors from the Syrian military announced a new military, the Free Syrian Army, aimed at toppling al-Assad's dictatorship. Minority groups continued to support al-Assad, while the country's Sunni Muslims sought his overthrow. Factions upon factions fought each other, Nezar told us, some with the added support of foreign governments, including the United States and Russia.

It was eerily dark when we reached Manbij, a city that, like Aleppo, had housed people from many religions and cultures: Kurds, Christians, Arabs, and people who followed the mystical Islam, Sufism. Now, the city seemed deserted. "We all lived peacefully," Nezar said, "until this bloody war. The prophet Muhammad entrusted his followers with neighbors of all faiths, and that included people not of the book."

We entered the apartment Nezar shared with his two sisters and his father. Framed pictures of Quranic verses covered the walls. One showed hands belonging to people of different skin colors linked together above a Quranic verse: *Good and evil deeds are not equal. Repel evil with what is better: then you will see that one who was once your enemy has become your dearest friend.*

"We're Muslim. But if you were confused by my Shingali, it's because my family were originally Yazidi," Nezar clarified.

We were shown to a guest room, where Nezar's sisters served us black tea and vanilla biscuits.

But I couldn't eat or drink.

One of Nezar's sisters asked if we wanted to bathe.

Navine nodded. But a shiver ran through me. I thought of al-Amriki staring at me as I showered and shook my head quickly.

The tiny apartment was sparse. The rug was well worn. A Quran sat on one shelf, candles and kerosene lamps on another. The kitchen at the far end of the guest room contained only the necessities: metal pots of various sizes, bowls, a fridge, and a gas stove. The two women were preparing rice and vegetables.

When the lights flickered and then went off, Nezar's sisters lit the kerosene lamps. At least they had had *some* electricity that day, they said. Daesh was trying to kick all the city's residents out by siphoning off the electricity and water. "It's getting harder and harder for us to stay in the city," one of the sisters said in frustration.

Nezar's father, sitting cross-legged and smoking the shisha pipe, said little, but I could tell he was listening intently.

"Why are you Muslim?" I asked Nezar as he lit up a cigarette.

"My great-great-grandfather was a Yazidi. We lived not far from Shingal in the early twentieth century," he said. "The Armenians, who were Christian, were fleeing west from the Ottomans, who wanted their territory. The Yazidi harbored some of the people fleeing the genocide against them. As a result, we got targeted, too. Some Yazidi, including my great-great-grandfather, converted to Islam to avoid being killed. My mother and father longed to be back among the Yazidi in Iraq. They even tried to return to Shingal before I was born, but the Yazidi elders said that because they had become Muslim, they couldn't. I mean, we could live there, but we were not welcome in the Yazidi community anymore. My parents raised me to speak Shingali and respect Yazidi traditions. But that is all."

My heart sank. Al-Amriki was right. I would not be welcomed back, like Nezar's family. "But your great-great-grandfather was forced to convert. He had no choice!"

Nezar sighed. "I'm telling you this because things are different now," he said. "If there is any blessing in this recent genocide, it's that the Yazidi are being forced to do things differently."

Nezar took his phone out and started punching in numbers. "Here," he said, passing me the phone. "Someone wants to speak to you."

Majida's voice, like a rose, blossomed on the other end. Both of us burst into tears. "We're waiting for you in

Kurdistan," she said in a shaky voice. "I'm with Khudher."
The phone crackled, then my brother Khudher's voice
came on.

"Badeeah, are you safe?"

"Yes," I said. My heart soared. It was like a sun above
me was finally shining. "Eivan, too," I said. "We're alive
and together."

When Majida came back on the phone, I turned my
head away from Nezar and his father. I didn't want them
to hear. "Majida, I was told Yazidi men . . ." I couldn't
finish. "Am I allowed back? Things happened to me." My
words came out jumbled, and Majida asked me to repeat
what I was saying.

I swallowed through the lump in my throat. "I heard
that if a girl was . . . you know . . ." I couldn't get it out.

Majida spoke reassuringly. "Badeeah, no. Baba Sheikh
and the Jevata Rohani have invoked a thousand-year-old
ceremony for cleansing and welcoming girls and women
kidnapped by Daesh back into the community. We all
want you back. Every one of us, including the elders
who survived."

My eyes closed, thinking of the Jevata Rohani, the
highest spiritual council in the Yazidi faith. Now I was
truly happy.

Then I realized there was something odd in what
Majida had said. "What do you mean *survived*?" I asked.
"Who is not there with you?"

The phone fell silent.

"Majida," I pleaded.

"Badeeah, just get here safely and we will talk more then."

"Now," I said, my voice raised. "I need to hear it all."

Majida cleared her throat, then explained that when Daesh separated us in Solakh, she was taken to Mosul, along with Hadil and most of the other unmarried girls from Kocho. Daesh had tried to sell Majida at a market. When Majida wasn't bought, Daesh moved her around, stopping in villages along the way, including Kocho. There, as Daesh pillaged the homes we had left behind, Majida crept off the bus and hid in a cupboard for days until she gained the courage to walk to the mountains at night.

"I got the idea of hiding from hearing you and Eivan talking," she said. "I'm so sorry I didn't pay attention that day. But Badeeah, if you and Eivan had hidden that day when Daesh came, they would have found you. Anyone left in the village, they killed."

The two of us cried together, and Majida finally said what I feared most: Fallah, Adil, Hadil, Hassan, Adlan, two more of my brothers, and an older sister were still missing. I clung to the phone and wept.

∽

Nezar woke us before dawn. Navine and Eivan put on new clothes, but I refused to change.

I didn't want to part with the dress I had worn when I left Kocho or the sweater I had knit with Dake. But I did accept an additional sweater, as well as new boots. Navine and I were also given new niqabs to wear.

Nezar explained that he was going to accompany us by bus to Turkey. He showed us Syrian identification papers belonging to his two sisters. If we were asked at checkpoints, he would say the papers were Navine's and mine. For Eivan, Nezar had purchased a fake Syrian passport.

It was 9:00 a.m. when the bus stopped not far from Nezar's apartment. The three of us followed him on board, standing well back as he gave the driver money for our tickets. We spread out on the bus for our safety. Nezar had explained that it was best to pretend we didn't know each other. That way, if one of us were caught, there was a chance the others could still continue on. As I walked to the back with Eivan, I could see that many travelers were crammed into their seats, buried under suitcases, boxes, bags, and babies. Passports and travel documents poked out of the pockets of the men's dishdashas and suits. Everyone, including the smallest of children, was carrying something.

I closed my eyes as the bus inched its way out of the city. I didn't want to look at Syria anymore. I didn't want any flashbacks of my earlier time on buses, drugged and floating across the desert, as the girls and women around me were sold as slaves.

At the checkpoints, I held my breath as the bus doors flew open. But Daesh never got on.

No one asked to buy us.

No one spat at us or called us sabaya.

Only when we reached Qamishli in the northeast did soldiers check our travel documents. But these soldiers were with another army. I didn't know which one.

ᐧᑕᕉ

Just before the Turkish border, most of the passengers piled out of the bus. I woke Eivan and put him down to walk on his own so we could both stretch our legs.

Pine and oak trees surrounded us. The air was fresh. I took off my khimar and niqab like some of the female refugees had done, closed my eyes, and tilted my bare face up toward the sun.

"We're still in Syria," I heard Nezar say after a minute. "We have to walk into Turkey from here through these woods."

I nodded. Nezar had warned us that if we were caught on the Syrian side of the border, we could be sent back to Aleppo. If we were caught in Turkey, we might be sent to jail. Turkey was not our final destination. But hundreds of thousands of Syrians were streaming into Turkey escaping the war, and the country had warned it couldn't handle all the refugees.

Some of the people who had been on the bus with us were already moving into the forest to make the perilous crossing. A light drizzle started to fall, dampening our clothes and sending a chill through me.

"Follow me," Nezar said, taking Eivan's hand. "I will lead you to the crossing. When I say go, we must run."

My feet crunched on dead twigs and thin pools of ice. The soft rain soon grew into a downfall.

The path through the trees was littered with discarded clothes, boxes, books, furniture, and even appliances. One by one, I watched as people let slip from their grasp everything but the essentials. I slowed my pace as we passed a doll with pink plastic skin, tangled hair, and coal-black eyes.

When we reached the crossing, one of the older refugee men took command, allowing only a few people to cross at a time. If we crossed all together, the noise might attract the border guards on either side.

Small children were to be carried, and everyone was to run as fast as they could.

"Have you done this before?" I asked Nezar nervously.

"Too many times," he replied.

We huddled together and waited our turn, soaked by the rain.

"Go," the man in charge finally directed us.

With Eivan's arms wrapped around my neck, I ran.

The mud beneath my feet was slippery. Down the incline I flew, losing sight of Navine and Nezar in the trees.

I was running faster than I could control, but it was too dangerous to stop.

My left foot got caught on a root hidden underneath dead leaves. I twisted through the air, still clutching Eivan, my body landing on the ground with a thump. As I skidded, my head hit a rock.

Nezar, breathless, rushed to my side. He helped Eivan up, then me. I felt dizzy, but Nezar hoisted Eivan into his arms and told me to keep running. I did what he said, willing my legs to keep up with Nezar.

When we reached the other side, we continued running down a dirt road. My chest hurt. My vision was blurred from the pain bolting through me.

The doors of a waiting truck flew open. Two men dressed in Yazidi-style clothing got out and waved for us to hurry. Nezar handed Eivan to one of the men. When I caught up to them, I was whisked into the back seat.

As the truck lurched forward, I passed out.

I awoke to find myself on a sofa in a small apartment. Nezar was kneeling over me, applying a cold compress to my pulsing head. I reached up and felt a bump the size of a duck egg.

I tried to sit up, but Nezar pushed me gently back down, saying we were at his aunt and uncle's place. "We're safe here. Rest."

"Where's Eivan?"

"In the other room, sleeping by the fire," he said.

Nezar's aunt shooed Nezar out of the room and helped me take a drink of water through a straw. She encouraged me to eat some naan. I would need the energy, she insisted. But I couldn't.

I lay back down and closed my eyes, listening to Nezar and his relatives talk. His uncle and aunt's house was small and sparsely furnished. It had been given to them, I heard Nezar tell Navine, by a kind person in their Turkish village. Like so many others, Nezar's relatives had had to abandon their jobs and their lives due to the Syrian civil war, fleeing with little to nothing.

I drifted off again, waking to find Navine asleep beside me. In the other room, Nezar was still talking to his uncle, telling him that he would be returning to Aleppo in the morning. I groggily pulled myself up and went to join them.

Nezar smiled when he saw me.

Nezar's uncle called out for his wife to bring us some tea and food.

Nezar was returning to Aleppo to rescue another Yazidi girl, I had heard him say.

"Are you safe doing this work?" I asked him.

He looked away and shook his head.

"Why do you do it, then?"

He shrugged. "I used to run a shop in Manbij. Then Daesh came, and my family faced a choice: Should we stay or leave? Some of us chose to stay and fight our own way, by rescuing Yazidi and helping refugees leave. The evil in this world can never be destroyed by the hatred that created it. Every person is a sister or a brother. When we really believe that, we're free."

Nezar's uncle stirred the chimney fire, tossing in some kindling to feed the flame. Nezar's aunt, the pleats of her long skirt dusting the floor the way Adlan's would, came into the room with a tray of tea, biscuits, fruit, honey, and bread.

Eivan stirred and called out for me. I crept over and pulled him into my arms.

Navine, awake now, entered the room to join us.

"I have good news," Nezar said as Navine sat down, curling her legs underneath her. "Eivan's mother is alive and in a refugee camp. I'm sure she's aching to see her son."

Navine turned to me. "Badeeah, what is Nezar saying? Eivan . . . he's not yours?"

I shook my head, realizing I had never told her. "I'm just an unmarried girl," I said.

"Who is he, then?" she asked, her face awash with surprise.

"My nephew. I'm just a teenager. I'm still a girl," I repeated as my eyes filled with tears. At least I had been a girl before al-Amriki. For the hundredth time since my abduction from Kocho, I thought about Nafaa.

"But you risked everything for Eivan!" Navine exclaimed.

Nezar smiled. "Now you know, Badeeah, why I do what I do. Life really begins when we start living for others."

∽

The others had gone to bed, but I found it hard to sleep.

Images of Kocho, of Dake's fruit trees and garden, of my mother cooking, of my father in our guest room rolling cigarettes and talking politics, of my school years and my cousins dancing came to me as sharp, painful images.

Eivan and I would not be going home, that much I knew. We would be joining Majida and Khudher at a refugee camp in Dohuk, Kurdistan. Kocho had been destroyed, I'd learned from Nezar, and anyway, it was still in Daesh hands.

Chapter Twenty-One

We're Not Afraid of Darkness

The next morning was cold. Frost lined the inside of the windowpanes. Outside, ice coated the brown grass and the boughs of the evergreen trees. The village was quiet except for a barking dog as we said goodbye to Nezar. A Yazidi man named Murad was taking us to Kurdistan. He arrived in an old car, silver and rusted along the bottom. I was wearing my own dress and sweater again, which had been cleaned.

The day turned bright as the car made its way up into the roads snaking through the mountains, capped in snow, that separated Turkey from Iraq.

My head still hurt from my fall the day before. By noon,

I had a blinding headache. But I didn't mind the pain. It meant I was still alive.

Eivan remained awake throughout the journey. Navine and Murad filled the quiet by humming folk songs. For long stretches, all of us were quiet, wondering what was to come next.

We stopped high on the Iraqi side of the mountains for tea, bread, tomatoes, and yogurt. I still could not eat, so I left the others to walk. The sky was clear, the sun warm on my face. For a moment, I felt peace move through me. I was back in my own country: a place I had feared I would never see again.

A heaviness fell over us as the car slowed and merged into traffic in the city of Dohuk, nestled in a large valley beside the Tigris River.

I peered out over Kurdistan. Modern buildings stood tall beside age-old stone complexes. Dohuk had been inhabited over the years not only by the Kurds but also Jews and Christians. Some people said Dohuk was a Yazidi name. The city had weathered many conflicts, Murad told us. Even the Ottomans had once laid claim to it.

Outside of the city, Murad turned the car onto a road muddy from the winter rains and full of potholes.

"Rwanga refugee camp," he said in a quiet voice.

I gazed out at the rows upon rows of trailers that Murad explained had been purchased by the Kurdish Rwanga Foundation.

Blankets stretched across windows, acting as curtains. Clotheslines drooped from the weight of frozen shirts, pants, and dresses. Dented metal pots hung from horizontal poles balanced atop outdoor fires. Tired-looking women, some young, some old, sat waiting for the flatbread they were frying to sizzle.

The camp housed many of the survivors from Kocho, Murad told us. There were now camps across Kurdistan for Syrian as well as Yazidi refugees. I shuddered. Rwanga might have been Kocho transplanted, but this was a place waiting for life to be breathed back into it.

As our sedan crawled through the maze of caravans, I searched for any faces I might recognize.

Most of the adults I could see were women. A dark shadow passed over me as I realized the men were still missing.

Children moved skittishly, traumatized by whatever they had lived through. I recognized trauma from the times I had helped out at the doctor's office. It was like a demon that burned inside its victims. None of us would ever be the same again.

∾

Murad parked his vehicle near a brick building that housed the offices of the United Nations. Beside the building was a caravan that had been converted into a traveling medical clinic. "We're going in there first," Murad said, pointing.

Warm air from a heater swept over us when we stepped inside, along with the pungent odors of disinfectant and medicines.

A woman in a black coat and pants and hair tied back into a loose, messy braid moved toward us. Her smile was wide and welcoming.

"I'm Sozan," she said, stopping in front of me. "You've come from Aleppo?"

I recognized Sozan's choppier and more guttural Kurdish dialect. Shingali is soft and also uses Aramaic words. Originally, the Yazidi spoke Akkadian. Sozan, I could tell right away, was not Yazidi. She was Kurdish, but our languages have much in common, so I could understand her.

Sozan was nearly half a foot taller than me.

"I'm Badeeah Hassan Ahmed," I said.

"Where are you from?" Sozan asked.

"Kocho."

A man and another woman appeared from a back room, both wearing white doctors' coats.

The man asked if he could examine Eivan. I didn't want anyone other than me touching him even though I knew he needed to be examined. But my permission was just a courtesy. The doctor took an unhappy Eivan. Sozan explained that the doctors weren't going to hurt him.

"They will make sure he's healthy. Give him antibiotics for dysentery and any other infections he might have." My eyes floated across the caravan. There were first aid bags, boxes of bandages, and shelves of medicines.

"Badeeah," Sozan asked, "what have you been told about Kocho?"

"Nothing," I replied in a barely audible voice.

As I looked at Sozan, Majida came into my mind. My sister had told us many times that Kurdish women had more freedoms than Yazidi girls, especially after the Americans came. Sozan looked close to my age and she was already working at the refugee camp. In another time, when I had dreams, I had wanted to help people, too.

"Kocho was hard hit," Sozan said quietly. "Of the 1,700 villagers, more than two-thirds are unaccounted for. We want to believe they're just trapped somewhere, unable to get out yet."

I could hear Eivan crying. A darkness swept over me. I heard Sozan say that someone had gone to get Majida and Khudher.

All of a sudden, though, I didn't feel like I was in the room anymore.

I lifted my right hand. I stared at it. I knew it was mine. I could see the tiny blue veins in my wrist pulsing through my pale skin. But nothing seemed real.

∾

I hear shuffling feet. Hands are touching me, leading me to a cot. I am being asked to lie down. Someone unties my boots. My socks are pulled off. My feet are swollen, I hear someone say, and blisters are popping. My body twitches under the sting of anesthetic. I hear the ripping apart of plastic bandages.

My sweater is unbuttoned. I feel a cool metal stethoscope sneaking down my chest.

My eyelids are pried open. A light is shone into them.

"Open your mouth?" someone asks. A flat wooden stick is placed on my tongue. I say "Ah."

"I was touched down there," I hear myself say.

"Tomorrow," the female doctor says. "There is a female doctor in Dohuk who will do a full examination, but it won't be until tomorrow or the next day."

Al-Amriki, *I keep thinking.* Where is he? Will he come and get me?

∽

And then I remembered al-Aamriki's phone. I sat up with a jolt. The doctor reached to pull me back down, but I leapt off the cot so fast she couldn't catch me. In the outer room, I found Murad. "I have something," I told him in a hoarse voice.

I pulled the cell phone from my pocket.

"I couldn't get it to work in Aleppo," I said, pushing the phone into Murad's hand. "It's his, the man who held us in captivity. He had other phones, too. Take it to the Peshmerga or the Americans, whoever is helping us. The man who took me, tell them, they called him the Sheikh of Aleppo. He was an emir."

Khudher and Majida got to the caravan just as Murad was putting the phone in his pocket. My brother and sister barreled into me. We wet each other's hair and cheeks with our tears. We touched each other's faces and shoulders, confirming that we were really there, that we were not dreaming anymore. We wept, too, for all the members of our family who were not with us.

Khudher and Majida spoke like a team, excited to have me home and to have an audience. I gathered that it had just been the two of them for a long time. Our married older sisters who had managed to escape Daesh lived in other camps with their husbands' families.

Navine's uncle had arrived to pick her up to live at a camp inhabited by survivors from her village. It seemed strange to be separated from her. We had been one beating heart for so long, I felt a part of me was being torn off when I watched her leave. As I watched the vehicle with Navine and her uncle slowly exit the camp, I heard Sozan say that Eivan would be staying with us until his mother, Samira, could arrange transportation to our camp.

Majida was open to talking about what had happened to her. But Khudher grew sober when I asked him. "I walked to Kurdistan," was all he would say. "I walked here."

The caravan Majida and Khudher were given was small. A worn Kurdish carpet that Majida had bought in a secondhand market in Dohuk covered part of the floor. The caravan had a small gas cooker and a tiny fridge. There was a shower, too, but the water, when it ran, was cold. Their pots, dishes, utensils, clothing, and bedding had either been donated or bought used in Dohuk, Majida told me. Anything we had owned in Kocho was still in Kocho or in Daesh's hands.

Once a month, the charity Khalsa Aid doled out sugar, vegetable oil, rice, and tomato paste to every household in the camp. The Yazidi there had also started to set up businesses, realizing they would not be returning to Kocho anytime soon. When she had arrived, there was nothing, Majida said. Now the road leading into the camp had shops selling clothes and mobile phones, vegetable and fruit shops, bakeries, butchers, and even a candy store. My heart fluttered, wondering if it was Nafaa's candy shop. But even if it was, he would not want me. Not anymore.

Khudher had applied for our father's pension from his job with the Kurdistan Democratic Party. With that money, Majida bought food Khalsa Aid didn't provide.

What was left over, the two of them saved in the hope that the rest of our family would find their way to us.

On my first night in the camp, before I could even settle in, Kocho visitors had streamed into our caravan to welcome me back. Women cried and pulled me into their arms. As I felt their tears washing over me, a floodgate of emotions was unleashed inside of me: joy at being reunited, fear that I would be taken again, and sadness, deep and painful, that so many Yazidi from Kocho were still missing. Always, the shame of what had happened to me twisted beneath the surface. I noticed I could not look at people the way I used to. When my eyes caught someone else's, I blushed and looked quickly away, as if all my secrets had been revealed. A part of me feared, despite being assured otherwise, I would be sent away if anyone discovered what al-Amriki had done to me.

Eivan's mother, Samira, arrived a few days later. She had evaded capture by hiding in the mountains, like she had told Fallah she was going to do. She had been living in a refugee camp with family and people from her village, Tal Banat.

She rushed into the caravan, her arms reaching for Eivan. But he clung to me, hiding behind my skirt. Samira shrunk back, stunned. Her only child was still calling me Mama.

The doctor who had examined us said Eivan was suffering from post-traumatic stress disorder. It could take months for him to heal, maybe longer, the doctor explained, since the camps' few psychologists were exhausted and were helping thousands of refugees in other camps as well. Almost everyone had experienced great loss. Samira, her face awash in sadness, was advised that Eivan should remain with me for another few weeks.

I was worried about Khudher, too. Majida had shown me a photograph of him when he first arrived at the camp. He was bare chested, his shoulder covered in bloody bandages. He claimed he had fallen in the hills when he was walking. But I didn't believe him. The more I was around my brother, the more I saw how sour he had turned. He was critical of the armies fighting Daesh, arguing they were not doing enough. "Daesh took our honor," he would huff. "They killed many Yazidi. They took our houses. We're in Kurdistan now, but Peshmerga didn't protect us. Our Arabic neighbors betrayed us. No one is helping us, not even America."

∾

A month passed, and the doctors felt Eivan and Samira finally needed to be together. Eivan screamed as his mother tugged at his wrist, clinging onto me even more tightly. I tucked my face into his hair and struggled to hold back my tears. We sat that way for a few minutes, but finally I could take no more of his cries.

"Eivan," I said. "I want to tell you a story. I need you to listen."

Startled, Eivan stopped squirming and looked at me intently.

"The day my grandmother died, I got very sick," I said. As I spoke, Dake's funeral flashed through my mind: the wailing women in black and all the mourners. "As the day wore on, my fever rose. I broke out in a rash, and I started to see strange things."

I could feel Eivan's body trembling. "Fallah, your father, was so worried about me that he called in sick to his police job, piled me into his truck, and drove me to Shingal to the hospital. I stayed there for days. No one could understand why I was sick." My voice trailed off as I remembered Fallah pacing the hallway outside my room. "I heard him crying when the doctors said they couldn't bring my fever down. He thought I was going to die.

"I fought my way back, then," I told Eivan. "I knew I had to live for him."

Eivan stayed quiet, but I knew he was listening.

"After Fallah returned from the Iraqi army," I continued, "he had lost a part of himself. But I saw the old Fallah return, that little spark in his eye and the warmth that spread out far and wide from his big, friendly heart. You and your mother were the light that helped him find his way home. Eivan, you need to go with your mother now because your father is in a dark place, like where we have just been. Do you understand?"

"Like Mir Meh," he eventually said, as he loosened his grip on my neck. "When he went down to earth and forgot about Falak?"

"Yes," I said. "You need to help your mother shine a bright light from your hearts so that Fallah can find his way back to you."

I wanted Eivan to stay with me. Like when Navine left, I felt as if a part of me was being cut away. But I needed to return him to his mother.

After a minute, Eivan climbed down from my lap. When he was standing in front of me, he asked me to put my hands out. I started to weave my fingers together, thinking we were going to play the finger game. "No, hands flat," he said. "Close your eyes."

I felt his little toy taxi being placed in my hand.

I opened my eyes to see Eivan walking slowly over to Samira, who pulled him into her arms and smothered him in kisses.

Chapter Twenty-Two

Return to Love

I had refused to go into Dohuk to be examined by the female doctor, making excuse after excuse when Sozan came. I didn't bathe, either. The water in the caravan was too cold, I said. I'd wait for hot water. I gripped my stomach often and moaned that I didn't feel well.

Every day, Khudher and Majida would leave, often right after waking, to get food from the shops and to help around the camp, bandaging the wounded, handing out the supplies the international community had sent in, or talking with staff and other refugees about how to find those still in Daesh's hands.

I liked it when they were gone, since there was nobody

to urge me out of bed, but at the same time, I found the quiet terrifying. I sat for hours on the Kurdish rug, my legs curled under me and a wool blanket, dotted with moth holes, draped over my shoulders. I thought about Navine. I wondered how she was adjusting to her new life. But most of the time, I thought about nothing at all. Remembering my family and my former life was too painful.

I waited to be returned to al-Amriki, to be recaptured. I braced myself for the sound of gunshots. With every dog bark, raised voice, or crackle from a fire, I worried Daesh had invaded the camp. The whole time I was awake, I seemed to hear the dripping of a leaking shower faucet, as if I were back in Aleppo. And I hated my body. Whenever I got up and walked around, I felt wounded, judged, and shamed.

Sozan came and sat with me from time to time. She'd talk in a gentle voice and I'd try to listen, but I'd eventually hear only white noise.

I longed to see my mother, but her voice, which had guided me in Raqqa, was gone. I was stuck in a caravan in a dark, dank refugee camp in the throes of winter.

One evening, at Sozan's urging, Majida and I talked about Mayan Khatun and how Yazidi women had been oppressed when she became Amira, or princess, but with Queen responsibilities, of the Yazidi in 1913. At the time, women were forbidden to make decisions, either in public life or in the home. Mayan Khatun was surrounded by men who at first would not listen to her. But she studied oppression, including its root causes. She saw that hate only begat more hate and fear begat more fear, and she used her observations to empower the Yazidi. She was the first woman to address men at the Jevata Rohani, the Yazidi spiritual council. She persisted in the face of dismissal and ridicule until finally the Yazidi realized she was right. Male and female principles had to balance one another. Families had to be strong. People needed to build their lives not on fear or anger but on love and respect. Mayan Khatun became the voice of revolution among the Yazidi people, in which female energy, Khatuna Fakhra, was allowed to rise and bring balance to society.

Majida took my hands in hers. "We are having a similar revolution now," she said. "All of us who were captured by Daesh have seen the purest of evil. Do you know that when Baba Sheikh addressed the leaders of our tribes, he said this Daesh genocide is the biggest test the Yazidi have faced in learning not to hate? This is our chance to show the universe we are good people. Badeeah, I know it hurts. I know there is great rage inside of you. I feel it, too. But the first step to healing is to bring that rage out into the light."

∾

"You need to shower," Sozan said to me one day. Her voice was stern. Another woman was with her, a Yazidi social worker named Sara from the charity WADI.

"Red Wednesday is coming," Sozan continued. "We're going to celebrate the New Year in the camps."

At the mention of celebration, I thought of Benyan and Nazma's wedding. Nafaa and I had linked arms to dance. Nafaa, who was still missing, along with Hassan, Fallah, Adil, Hadil, Adlan . . . all of them had been at the wedding. The air had been filled with the sounds of laughter and conversation, our music and our dreams.

I felt my stomach twisting. A fury buried deep inside of me began to rise. Like a demon, it flew up and took hold of my body.

I leapt to my feet, growled, and raised my fist to hit Sozan.

Instead of cowering, though, she held up a pillow. "Punch, kick, anything . . . just start getting it out," she encouraged me.

I looked away not knowing what to do.

"Badeeah, we need to move your healing along now," Sara said in a soft voice. "It's time you came back to join the living."

The *drip, drip, drip* of al-Amriki's shower filled my head. I smacked my hands over my ears to block it out.

Suddenly, it all came rushing back. Every blow, every bruise, every abusive word from al-Amriki.

"Please leave me alone," I said to Sozan and Sara. My voice seemed to come from somewhere very far away.

Sara shook her head. "No," she said. "We need to make sure you're safe."

I could take no more of these two. My patience had worn out. I bolted for the door of the caravan.

When Sozan stepped in front of me, I let out a piercing scream. I began to spin around, with my eyes closed and my hands clawing at my arms and legs. I wanted to get rid of whatever evil was inside of me.

"Let it all out," Sozan said. "Don't run away from what's inside of you. Bring it into the light."

Finally, I crumbled to the ground, sobbing. "I curse you, al-Amriki," I shouted. "You are the one without true faith, not me."

After a few minutes, I could hear myself breathing. But there was no more dripping sound. I no longer heard the leaking shower faucet.

I sat up, pulling my knees into my chest. "The man who took me said Yazidi men would hate me for what he did to me. The man said I would not be welcomed back."

Sara took my hand. "Baba Sheikh has welcomed everyone's return. For us women and girls, he invoked a thousand-year-old prayer to ease our suffering. You're safe now, Badeeah. Our people do not judge you for what you have been through. You are not as your captors defined you."

"But I became his wife. He tricked me to make me Muslim." I pushed the words out as if they were stuck deep inside me. My eyes filled with tears as I thought of Nafaa. "I wanted to marry someone else one day, after I returned to school."

"Badeeah," Sozan said. "It is a war crime, not love. Not a marriage. And he forced you to convert to Islam, so rest your fears. Your spiritual elders have already acknowledged that you and the others did nothing wrong."

In the shower room, I took off my sweater and folded it neatly. Next came my dress, my pants, and finally my undergarments. I set out a white towel before ducking underneath the running water. The water was finally hot. The soap I held in my hand smelled like vanilla.

Chapter Twenty-Three

Giving

We celebrated New Year's in the caravan, eating dolma and kubbeh that Majida, Samira, and I had prepared together. For the first time in a long time, I enjoyed buying ingredients and cooking. As we cooked, Majida talked about the all-female Yazidi battalion led by Khatoon Khider. One of the first women to publicly perform Yazidi music had formed a small army to fight Daesh and help rescue Yazidi girls and women. "We don't have Mayan Khatun among us, but we all can be her," Majida said. "We can lead a revolution like she did but this time make our voices heard so that women and girls don't slip back into a cycle of oppression."

So many Yazidi women and girls were almost illiterate. What we needed was knowledge. A few days later, I told Sozan that I wanted to return to school. I still wanted to study medicine, but first I needed to get my high school diploma. Some governments, she told me, including Germany, were taking in girls like me, helping us with our psychological problems and offering education. I told her I'd have to think about that. I didn't want to leave my family, not yet. A part of me knew my mother, father, and brothers had been killed. But another part of me needed to believe they were still alive. Eivan and Samira had moved in with us. Most of the time, I felt warm inside as I watched them cuddle and talk. But every now and then, something deeper and uglier tugged at me. In those moments, I missed being that close to Eivan. He had been my lifeline during our time in captivity, after all. But in Eivan's eyes, I was his aunt again.

I forced myself to keep busy, even though I still tired easily. I'd head out with Khudher and Majida to the shops and to visit with new arrivals. I volunteered with Sozan, sorting donated food items into bags and boxes that went to Khalsa Aid. Every week, the camp expanded as more Yazidi found their way to us. Every day, traumatized girls and women arrived.

Green returned to the land as the trees gave birth to new leaves and grass started to sprout. Soon the scent of roses and orange blossoms filled the camp.

I met often with Sozan and Sara, who taught me that healing was a journey of self-discovery. "Demons only scare us when they're hidden," Sara explained. "Healing is like peeling an onion, finding those demons that keep us stuck. Just when one is found and discarded, another one appears underneath. But eventually, for those brave and determined, what lies at the very bottom is love and light."

With every piece of my story I dug out for them, I felt chunks of darkness leaving me.

One afternoon, Sozan asked if I would speak to the Yazidi girls and women who had come back. Many were like I had been when I first arrived: lost, full of shame, confused, and hurting. None of them wanted to speak about their ordeals at first.

I said I wasn't ready. I still felt hate and anger, I told her, and often asked myself why I had lived when so many others were missing or dead. Why did I deserve life more than them?

"Maybe it's time you visited Lalish and did the ceremony with Baba Sheikh to cleanse you of your suffering. You can honor your family, too," Sara suggested. "Women and girls throughout our history have lived with pain, Badeeah. Go to Lalish and connect with them."

Despite Sara's words, guilt churned inside me. Finally, after a day when negative thoughts plagued me, I prayed to Khatuna Fakhra.

When I was done, the caravan was pitch-black. Night had fallen outside. I could still hear the voices of children playing, though, and a mother calling for her son to come eat. A newborn cried. Two women bickered over something I couldn't make out.

As I lay down to sleep, I heard my mother's voice. "Dream again, Badeeah. Be wiser and fiercer than you ever were before. Love is the greatest weapon against hate."

The next morning, as I walked to my volunteer job in the clothing shop, I realized something had changed. Instead of seeing only sorrow and horror in the eyes of the children and women I passed, I now saw hope. I had been looking only at losses. Now I vowed to celebrate what we still had. "Our love is bigger than your hate," I said, at first softly and then more strongly. People I passed stared, but I kept on repeating the phrase like a mantra. "Our love is bigger than your hate."

That very afternoon, I spoke to my first group of returning girls and women. I was nervous at first. The women and girls could not look me in the eye. They hunched their bodies tightly together. Their essence seemed to be elsewhere, adrift, on a vast sea. I knew what they had been through. I was determined to offer them the rope they needed to start coming back. That rope was reassuring them they were not alone, they were welcome back, and most of all, they were loved.

After that, I met with the new arrivals every week, sharing my story and listening to theirs, although few were ready to share what they had been through, even with me.

Chapter Twenty-Four

Freedom

After one of our meetings with a group of girls and women, Sozan told me that she had been acting as a translator for foreign media. CNN, BBC, and *The New York Times* wanted to interview women who had been abducted by Daesh. Other than my cousin Nadia, who was living at the same camp as me, few of the girls and women were willing to tell their stories. Was I ready to share mine? Sozan asked.

At first, I hesitated. As Yazidi, we are raised to be private about our lives. Our elders believed the first genocides we faced came after we shared our spirituality and mysticism with non-Yazidi. Our enemies had become afraid or jealous of our power and control. Over time, the Yazidi began to share little to nothing about ourselves with the outside world. Our privacy was protection, or so we thought.

Just a few days earlier, Helly Luv had released a new single called "Revolution." Majida had dragged me out to an electronics shop so we could listen to it on the radio.

As Sozan waited for my answer, I sang the chorus of the song silently to myself. After a few seconds, I knew I would do it. Being brave meant facing our fears, like Mayan Khatun had. The world needed to know what had happened to the Yazidi. The time had passed where keeping our culture secret gave us safety.

The first journalist I spoke with was a Kurdish woman from a local newspaper. I could converse with her in Shingali. Her questions revolved around the massacre at Kocho. I cried as I recounted being driven out of town by the boy soldier, my eyes glued to the front door of my house. But she didn't ask me about Aleppo.

An interview with a Middle Eastern newspaper followed. I surprised myself by feeling comfortable as a spokesperson. My reservations about speaking publicly quickly disappeared.

But then an English-speaking woman with straw-blonde hair and bright blue eyes came into the caravan where the interviews were taking place.

My body stiffened, and my stomach started to churn. I fought the instinct to run out of the room.

"Are you American?" I stammered.

"Yes," the woman replied.

Her accent sounded the same as al-Amriki's. My knees shook under the table.

The American journalist started to ask me questions. I recited the answers as if on autopilot. Al-Amriki's face and that of the blonde woman on the computer flashed in front of me every time the journalist spoke.

"Can you tell me more about the man in Aleppo who bought you?" said Sozan, translating for the journalist. In Kurdish, Sozan added that I didn't need to talk about my abductor if it distressed me.

While I had told Sozan, Sara, and Majida almost everything about my abduction, I had left out one important detail: that my captor was an American. I'd never used the term *al-Amriki* to describe him. I didn't know why. Maybe I was still finding it too hard to reconcile how a nation I had looked to as one who grants freedoms could also take them away.

"He was like you," I said to the journalist.

Nightingale. I heard a nightingale singing.

Day, however, didn't turn to night, like it had on

August 15 with that sandstorm. Outside, it was still bright summer.

"He was one of you," I repeated.

The journalist said something to Sozan. "She doesn't understand," Sozan translated. "What do you mean when you say, 'He was one of you'?"

"He was American," I said. "Al-Amriki. He was like her." I pointed to the journalist. "He was white. He talked on the computer to a woman. She had a baby."

The journalist spoke rapidly to Sozan.

"Can you tell her anything else about him?" Sozan translated.

"Yes," I said, my voice rising. A confidence was growing inside me. "I listened in on al-Amriki's conversations with the soldiers who visited him." Now I wanted justice. If I could help stop Daesh and find our missing girls and women, I would. "They called him the Sheikh of Aleppo," I continued. "I overheard his plans, Daesh's plans for Syria. Every day or two, new guns would arrive. Al-Amriki seemed to be in charge of deciding which guns Daesh would buy."

The journalist asked me to wait while she made a phone call. A sketch artist accompanying the journalists' delegation soon joined us, and I told him what I remembered about al-Amriki's appearance. I recalled every terrible detail of his face. When the sketch was completed, I shivered. It was a strong likeness, except the artist made my captor seem larger than he actually was. Something lifted inside me. I felt freer.

With his likeness on paper, it was as if al-Amriki was no longer stuck deep inside me.

∾

I went to visit Navine at the Kabarto refugee camp. I had been missing her, but as soon as I laid eyes on her, a sadness swept through me. I felt my healing come crashing down around me. Seeing her brought back the entire ordeal, from the beatings and the girls being sold in Raqqa to our imprisonment and abuse in Aleppo.

I knew there would always be a thread that tied us together. But I wasn't ready to be with Navine yet.

When I returned to Rwanga camp, I headed straight for Sozan's office. I wanted to ask her if what had happened during my visit with Navine was normal. She told me it was. I might have these flashbacks for the rest of my life, she said. But in time, I would learn to recognize them for what they were: reminders of a past that was over.

As it turned out, Sozan had been looking for me while I was gone. A group called the International Organization on Migration was interested in flying me to the United States to speak about the Yazidi genocide, she said. If I went, the TV network CNN also wanted me to come to their New York studio. The US government was hunting through files for al-Amriki, and so far, they could not figure out who he was.

I didn't need to think about this request. I agreed immediately to go to America. I wanted people there to know what was happening to us Yazidi.

∾

For my trip to the United States, I needed to get new identity papers and a passport.

While I waited for the documents to be processed, the end of Chilé Haviné neared. It was almost one year since the invasion of Kocho.

Majida, Khudher, Samira, and I decided to go to Lalish to pray. We wanted to honor the lives of our family members who were still missing and presumed dead. I also planned to take part in the ritual Baba Sheikh was performing, along with our next highest spiritual leader, Baba Chawish, to help us heal from the psychological effects of abduction.

In the past, our pilgrimages to Lalish had been like parties, with dozens of us squeezing into a few cars. We made food to take with us, and we spent a lot of time getting ready, primping, posing, singing, and dreaming about the dancing we'd do.

This time, though, we were sober. Our transportation was a public bus. Our only treats were chocolates that we bought on the way out of the refugee camp at the sweet shop. Khudher went into the shop for us. I couldn't bear to look at the candies. They reminded me too much of Nafaa and of our captivity.

As the bus drew close to Lalish, Khudher started to sob. Majida moved to one side of him. I sat on the other. We rubbed his back and looped our fingers through his, waiting for him to speak.

"I was with the men . . . I was taken with the men," he said eventually in a strained voice. My lips started to quiver. After all these months of quiet, a part of me didn't want my brother to talk about what had happened to him.

"Our great-uncle Saleh, Dake's brother, was with me," he continued. "Daesh marched us out of town, to the Sur." The Sur was where we collected earth to make bricks for our houses. No matter how dry our summers were, the Sur was always muddy, the ground a shallow pool of water.

"Then a big man appeared. Bigger than the rest."

I shivered. "In a brown dishdasha?" I interrupted. Khudher nodded. The man must have been the Saudi Arabian, from the classroom.

"Daesh soldiers ordered us to get down on our knees and duck our heads. There must have been forty of us. The big man ordered his soldiers to shoot. I was shot here." Khudher lifted his shirt and showed Majida and me the scar: red and chafed, but healing.

"You told us you got that wound from falling," Majida whispered.

"Saleh was badly hurt in the shooting, but he ordered me to play dead. He rolled his body on top of mine to hide me. I heard women and girls screaming as the cars and trucks took you away. Then, when I heard nothing, I pushed Saleh's body off me. Keche, from our village, was alive, too, as was Elias, the doctor. The three of us made it to Mount Shingal. We hid there until we felt it was safe."

My eyes were closed, taking this all in. My heart ached.

"Before we walked into Kurdistan," Khudher was saying, "we returned to Kocho. There was no food left in the homes. Daesh had gone through everything, stealing anything they could sell. What they left behind was a mess: couches and pillows ripped open, cupboard doors pulled from their hinges, clothes strewn everywhere. Elias, Keche, and I walked to Piske next. We went to Jasim Abdulah's house. He answered the door, but he wouldn't let us in. He cried and said he couldn't help us. These men weren't just our friends, they were like our family," Khudher choked out. "They could have stopped it all."

Jasim, like Abu Anwar, had been loved by many people in Kocho. He had visited my father, Hassan, prayed in our guest room, eaten our food, and drunk Adlan's tea. I balled my fists together. I was deeply angry at those men, too.

∾

On our past pilgrimages to Lalish, we'd arrived to a cacophony of sound: music from the flute, framed drums and tamburs, the joyous squeals of friends and family reuniting, men helping each other unload food and supplies, the crackling of fires.

Not this time. Not a year after the massacre of our people.

In what had become a habit, I scanned the faces of those who had arrived in Lalish searching for Nafaa, Fallah, Adil, Hassan, Hadil . . . and for Adlan.

Majida passed me a Chira. I lit it and followed her and Khudher into the main temple, where the tomb of the twelfth-century mystic Sheikh Adi was located. I'd visited this place in my mind many times when I was in captivity. Now, I felt I had come home.

After we'd rested in the sun, Majida joined me for a private meeting with Baba Sheikh and Baba Chawish. I was nervous. What if they told me I had to leave the community? I reached over to grip Majida's arm. Under her breath, she reminded me, "Khatuna Fakhra."

Both leaders wore calm expressions. Baba Chawish asked about my family and about who was here with me.

"Badeeah," he then said, "your soul is advancing. Hatred is only a stone on your path to reach the fourth mind, the most advanced stage, or angel stage. Your love is stronger than hate."

I started to cry then, sobbing like a baby.

Baba Chawish leaned forward. "Dear girl, you did nothing wrong. You don't need forgiveness. Stay connected to the good power of the universe. In time, you will heal and feel the power of good running through you again."

After that, we prayed together.

When our meeting was over, Baba Chawish accompanied me to the White Cave, where some of the Faqras, the girls and women who dedicate their lives to spirituality, Lalish, and advancing their own souls, had already gathered. Baba Chawish had me kneel down. I dipped my hands into the water of the sacred spring and then drew them across my face, dampening my skin. The Faqras splashed water on me as Baba Chawish said another prayer.

The final part of the ceremony involved me changing into a white dress made from fabric from the same tree used for Baba Sheikh and the Faqras' robes and that we used to wrap the Berat. The belt they gave me was red, signifying love.

At first, I felt nothing.

But then out of nowhere, I had a vision. I saw Adlan. She was standing in front of me, wearing white and, this time, a red belt like mine. She held her hands out toward me, and at that moment, I knew Khatuna Fakhra had always been with me. She had guided me in the form of a butterfly when I was little and lost in Lalish. She was my mother, Navine, my sisters, and all the women and girls abducted by Daesh. She was all of us, and she was watching over us at the same time.

∽

Khudher and Majida had set up a place for us to eat and sleep under a large mulberry tree. Samira boiled water for tea. Eivan was playing with his football. As I returned from the White Cave, he came running up to me on stocky legs that were growing fat from Samira's love and cooking. I sat down on a stone and drew him into my lap.

"Maybe it's time for a story," I said. "Maybe I should tell you how the Samaran story ends?"

Eivan nodded eagerly.

"So the king's men find Samaran, the snake," I began. "She tells them that if the king eats her tail, he will inherit her immortality and wisdom. If he eats her head, he will die. But it's a trick. When the men kill Samaran and the king eats her tail, instead of gaining everlasting life, he dies. When Tasmasp stumbles upon her body, heartbroken, thinking he caused her death, he eats some of her head, wanting to die himself. He felt he had betrayed her. But do you know what?"

"What?" Eivan said. His eyes danced in the glow of the surrounding cooking fires.

"He didn't die. Tasmasp was the one who lived forever and inherited Samaran's wisdom. In her love for Tasmasp,

Samaran lived on. Some believe that Tasmasp is still alive, working as a doctor, healing people."

Eivan and I fell quiet as we listened to some older women singing. "Eivan," I whispered after a while. "Samaran isn't a Yazidi story. Let me tell you something we believe." He nodded.

"At Lalish, we enter the temple where Sheikh Adi's tomb is located through Mir Gate," I began. "Beside the door, if you remember, is a replica of a giant black snake. Way back, humanity faced a big flood. A ship was built and Noah brought two of each animal on board to save them. The ship had a hole. The entire vessel was sinking from one tiny leak, but a black snake slipped its body into the hole, blocking it up. The black snake we never kill because it saved the world."

Eivan was too young to know that in Aleppo, seeping through a giant hole inside me, was all my hope. I had nearly given up, sinking the both of us. Sometimes my thoughts still became so heavy, they almost drowned me. But I was determined that I would live an enlightened life, letting love guide me out of any darkness and toward the light. That's how we win. Love is how we defeat our enemies.

Epilogue

A Cave in the Clouds is based on the true story of Badeeah Hassan Ahmed. We have taken some creative license in telling the story, however, including recreating dialogue, combining some characters, and simplifying events for readers.

After Badeeah was captured and then separated from her sisters and her mother in Solakh, a distant relative recognized her in Tal Afar. That relative, who had converted to Islam, told Daesh that Badeeah was his son's wife and Eivan was his grandson. Badeeah and Eivan lived with the relative for about a month before Daesh militants recaptured them. Badeeah was eighteen when she was abducted.

The location in Raqqa depicted in the story is a composite of several locations where Badeeah was held prisoner. Daesh took over houses, schools, and factories in the places they invaded and used them as prisons for their sabaya. Before being sold to al-Amriki, Badeeah and Eivan were enslaved in a number of places in multiple cities and towns. Some of these were houses hiding only a few women and girls. Other places saw Badeeah and Eivan imprisoned with hundreds of Yazidi.

It was in Solakh, not Raqqa, that Badeeah met the guard who tried to save her.

Navine is a real person, although her name has been changed to protect her identity. She and Badeeah met in one of the Iraqi locations, not in Raqqa. Their experiences together and the bond they made in captivity are all real.

Sadly, Nezar, the human smuggler, died not long after rescuing Badeeah. She was informed he died at the hands of Daesh, who had infiltrated the rescue operations.

Hadil and Majida are composite characters combining the traits of several of Badeeah's sisters.

Badeeah's mother, father, all of her older brothers, including Adil and Fallah, are still missing. So is Nafaa. Mass graves have been discovered in Iraq, including one in Kocho that holds the remains of about seventy bodies. Another mass grave has been found in Solakh. The people buried in these graves have yet to be identified.

Today, Badeeah lives in Germany with Eivan and his mother, Samira. She is studying languages and nursing. Her dream is to become a nurse or a doctor to help her people.

Acknowledgments

From Badeeah

I want to thank Sozan Fahmi. Without her, I would not have been able to translate my story. You are my best friend and confidante and I owe so much to you. I also want to thank the Jinda and Wadi foundations that not only helped me but so many Yazidi girls and women. I want to thank Khalsa Aid for giving the opportunity to work and find a purpose in life again after my ordeal with ISIS. Thank you, Germany, for opening your borders to me and all of us Yazidi suffering from genocide. In particular, thank you to Manuela Zendt, Julia, Claudia, Wintus, Zika, Dr. Michael Blume, Dr. Jan Ilhan Kizilhan, and Mirza Ali Dinnayi.

Thank you to *Marie Claire* UK, who initially told my story; my brother and sisters who survived and who inspire and guide me every day; Dakhil Shammo and Imad and Fawaz Farhan, who provided invaluable information, translation, and understanding of my story and the Yazidi people.

Thank you to Nafiya Naso for writing the book's foreword.

To the real "Navine," without whom I would not have survived my time with ISIS. She helped save Eivan and me. I owe you my life.

To my spiritual elders, entire community, and especially the energy of Khatuna Fakhra. To the Yazidi spiritual leader, Baba Sheikh, without your decision, rescued girls like me would not have had the courage to come back and integrate in the community again.

I want to thank the human smugglers who helped me escape ISIS, particularly Nezar, who sacrificed his life to help Yazidi girls and women. He was killed not long after he rescued me.

To all of the people who have helped the Yazidi, thank you.

Finally, thank you, Susan McClelland, for writing my book with me and Annick Press for publishing my story. Thank you to all the readers who took the time to learn a little more about the beauty of the Yazidi people and our enduring courage.

From Susan

This book would not have been possible without the generous support of Sozan Fahmi, who works with Khalsa Aid and the WADI (Association for Crisis Assistance and Development Cooperation) and Jinda foundations in Dohuk, Kurdistan. Since Badeeah's rescue from Daesh, she and Sozan have become close friends. Together Sozan and I have weathered many storms and setbacks in making the stories of Yazidi women public. Tirelessly, Sozan has inspired me not to give up.

Dakhil Shammo and Nasir Kiret assisted greatly by clarifying the politics leading up to Daesh's invasion of Iraq and helping me to understand Yazidi life and culture. Thank you!

The insights into Yazidi spirituality in the book were made possible through the contributions of Imad Farhan and his father, the esteemed Yazidi author Fawaz Farhan. The trust they placed in me and the revelations they provided were rare and invaluable. *A Cave in the Clouds* is one of only a few English-language books that provide a glimpse into one of the oldest religions, faiths, and cultures on the planet. The Yazidi wisdom, its mysticism, its balance of male and female energies, and its faith that love is ever present inside us and in the universe must be preserved.

All Islamic references were fact-checked and approved by the scholar Khalid Aboulela. I extend many thanks to my lifelong friend and guide.

Thank you to Nafiya Naso for writing an insightful and compassionate foreword for the book. The work done by Operation Ezra is essential in addressing the plight of the Yazidi people.

I acknowledge Brooks Newmark and Nazim Baksh for their help fact-checking details about the war in Syria.

I wish also to thank Rick Wilks and the team at Annick Press. Rick has been a constant supporter of this type of creative non-fiction over the years, recognizing the importance of these narratives and the power of marketing and publicizing accounts like this one that touch and inform young readers around the world. For Barbara Pulling, my thoughtful editor, who also worked with me on *The Bite of the Mango*, I have nothing but praise and admiration. As I say to my children, praise is wonderful, but critique is better. Honor the person whose path it is to help you see where you are blind. Barbara, you take my words and these stories and make them great. I would also like to thank the Ontario Arts Council for their generous support.

Finally, Badeeah. What can I say? I think of you as a sister, a friend, a soul mentor. You are truly one of the special ones, the enlightened ones on this earth. The expansiveness of your heart and your generosity humble me and remind me of the goodness that can prevail over the darkest evils of humanity. The world needs to dance to the beat of your rhythm, girl!